Nonfiction
in Motion

Nonfiction in Motion

Connecting Preschoolers with
Nonfiction Books through Movement

Julie Dietzel-Glair

Chicago 2016

Julie Dietzel-Glair is a freelance writer and library consultant. She is the author of *Books in Motion: Connecting Preschoolers with Books through Art, Games, Movement, Music, Playacting, and Props* and the coauthor of *Get Real with Storytime: 52 Weeks of Early Literacy Programming with Nonfiction and Poetry*. She uses her years of experience as a children's librarian and assistant children's services coordinator to provide training sessions for librarians and other early literacy providers. She is active in the Association for Library Service to Children.

© 2016 by the American Library Association

Extensive effort has gone into ensuring the reliability of the information in this book; however, the publisher makes no warranty, express or implied, with respect to the material contained herein.

ISBN: 978-0-8389-1468-7 (paper)

Library of Congress Cataloging-in-Publication Data
Names: Dietzel-Glair, Julie, 1976- author.
Title: Nonfiction in motion : connecting preschoolers with nonfiction books through movement / Julie Dietzel-Glair.
Description: Chicago : ALA Editions, an imprint of the American Library Association, [2016] | Includes bibliographical references and indexes.
Identifiers: LCCN 2016018000 | ISBN 9780838914687 (paper)
Subjects: LCSH: Children's libraries—Activity programs. | Libraries and preschool children. | Preschool children—Books and reading. | Children's literature—Bibliography.
Classification: LCC Z718.3 .D55 2016 | DDC 027.62/5—dc23 LC record available at https://lccn.loc.gov/2016018000

Book design by Kimberly Thornton in Helvetica Neue and Minion Pro.
Cover images © Shutterstock, Inc.

⊚ This paper meets the requirements of ANSI/NISO Z39.48–1992 (Permanence of Paper).

Printed in the United States of America
20 19 18 17 16   5 4 3 2 1

contents

introduction / vii

introduction

Storytime is a magical experience for everyone involved. The combination of picture books, rhymes, and songs brings a smile to the face of a child and joy to the heart of every early literacy provider. Storytime is also the foundation for library service to preschool children and their parents. It is the perfect way to showcase quality books and model the five practices for early literacy. This book is designed to make storytime even more special by recommending nonfiction titles suitable for a preschool crowd and movements to enhance the experience of listening to those books.

Fiction picture books can make us smile, laugh, cry, and think. They can bring us to worlds stranger than the depths of our imagination. They can evoke a strong sense of nostalgia for adults who see a childhood favorite on a library shelf. It's no wonder that these books are the cornerstone of storytime. But what about nonfiction titles? Do they have a place in storytime? Yes, they do! They bring knowledge and information about the real world. They feed the desire for facts and photographs. Like fiction picture books, they can bring us to new worlds; while these worlds are real, some can still seem stranger than our imagination.

It is important to remember that informational reading can also be fun. Scatter a few nonfiction books in your storytime planning and help plant the seeds for a lifelong love of reading in kids who prefer fact over fiction. Including nonfiction books in storytime is especially important because of their appeal to boys who want books with "true stuff." As boys grow up, if they have developed of love of reading, you will often find them reading nonfiction.

Just adding nonfiction books to storytime can be enough, but I propose taking the excitement up a notch by adding movement while you read the book to a group. Including movement, art, music, or props is a simple way to touch on different learning styles in storytime. Some kids enjoy sitting quietly while a book is read to them, but many kids feel the need to move. Just think about the number of adults you know who doodle or fidget in a business meeting—and they've had years of practice in learning how to sit still and listen. Let's connect with those kinesthetic learners or musical preschoolers by supporting their learning style while introducing them to books. As an added bonus, you will feel a renewed excitement for your programs as you play with and explore nonfiction books with your storytime crowd.

About This Book

This book follows a similar format to *Books in Motion: Connecting Preschoolers with Books through Art, Games, Movement, Music, Playacting, and Props* (ALA Neal-Schuman, 2013); however, I incorporated a few key changes. *Books in Motion* features five hundred titles suitable for preschoolers. A majority of the books highlighted in *Books in Motion* are fiction titles; all were found in the picture book section of a public library. *Nonfiction in Motion* features two hundred titles suitable for preschoolers. Every title in this book is cataloged as nonfiction by the Library of Congress.

You may wonder why there are fewer titles. Simply put, the quality of nonfiction titles for children has come a long way, especially with the advent of awards like the Robert F. Sibert Informational Book Medal, sponsored by the Association for Library Service to Children. However, they still cannot compete in quantity with the sheer number of amazing fiction picture books published each year.

In *Books in Motion*, each title was filed under one of six different movement styles (art, games, movement, music, playacting, and props) to correspond with the suggested action. In *Nonfiction in Motion*, most of the entries boast two or three different suggested movements; they could not be classified under one movement style. Therefore, the books are grouped under five general topics. In chapter 1, "Animals," you will find everything from the cute and cuddly to the small and creepy. There are books about specific animals, like brown bears, beetles, or bumblebees. There are also books that feature many different animals and animal behavior. Chapter 2, "Concepts," features books about the alphabet, colors, counting and math, emotions, the five senses, and opposites. Every kid loves big trucks and construction equipment and, chapter 3, "Construction and Things That Go," has them all. You'll also find bicycles, helicopters, and trains. (Don't miss the explosions.) Chapter 4, "Science," boasts informational books about environmental science, food and how it grows, plants, space travel, and weather. You'll also find dinosaurs and eggs in this chapter; they could have been placed in "Animals," but they either no longer exist or aren't quite animals yet. "The World around Us" is the last chapter. Here you will find things in a child's everyday life as well as things to broaden their knowledge of the world. Topics include family, health and exercise, manners, music and dance, and occupations.

All the entries list identifying information for the nonfiction title; a brief summary of the book; and one, two, or more suggested movement activities (actions) that can be done while reading the book to preschool children. The goal of the multiple suggestions is to give you options—it is not expected or recommended that you do all the suggested movement activities for a book in a single storytime. However, you may wish to repeat the book the following week in order to try something else. You will also find occasional extension activities that can be done at the end of storytime to enhance the children's enjoyment of the topic.

Nonfiction in Motion concludes with an appendix of ten outlines for art projects. Refer to this section when a movement suggestion recommends a specific coloring sheet. You will also a find an index by author, an index by storytime subject, and an index by title. The storytime subject index provides ideas under general storytime themes. You will find titles that go beyond a specific topic but may fit with your storytime idea. For example, a book titled *Fireflies* is included under the "Bedtime" theme; the recommended book is not about bedtime, but is about an animal that is frequently spotted close to a child's bedtime.

The nonfiction section of libraries includes factual books, poetry, folklore, and fairy tales. There are many wonderful poetry books, folklore, and fairy tale options available for children; however, the purpose of *Nonfiction in*

Motion is a focus on facts. It is geared to help attract kids who like "true stuff" to storytime and books. Also, in hopes that the books will still be available for purchase or easily located on a library shelf, all the titles in this book were published in 2005 or later. Special consideration was given to accuracy in factual information presented in the highlighted titles at the time this book was written. I apologize if any scientific breakthroughs are made in the future that falsify information provided in these books.

Incorporating the Five Practices

Keep the five practices for early literacy in your mind whenever you are planning a program for preschoolers. Most early literacy providers include the acts of talking, writing, reading, playing, and singing in programs automatically. Help caregivers include these practices at home by mentioning them and providing tips.

For example, encourage parents to engage children in conversation while reading books with them; this helps children learn to understand and speak words. With nonfiction books, a caregiver can discuss with their child what page they liked best in the book and why. Encourage caregivers to incorporate what they learn in books throughout their day. For example, if they read a book about construction equipment with their child and then pass a building site later that day or week, they can talk about the cranes and bulldozers.

The practice of writing does not mean formulating an essay in one of those little blue books. Writing for preschoolers involves strengthening the muscles in the hands by scribbling with a crayon. Writing also includes increased letter recognition through tracing letters in the sand or on paper. Alphabet books with clear, uncluttered letters are wonderful nonfiction books that can be used for tracing letters by little fingers.

The simple act of reading builds a child's vocabulary; many people don't realize just how rich of a vocabulary is included in children's books. When kids have an interest in a particular topic (dinosaurs, reptiles, weather), nonfiction books are filled with topic specific vocabulary words. Remember that no one thinks twice about teaching kids dinosaur names, and those are very difficult words. Give an explanation using other words if a child is confused about particular vocabulary, but don't feel that you need to water down the text of a nonfiction book.

Playing helps children think symbolically. Pretend along with books to help kids put their thoughts into action. Even very young children like to talk about what they are going to be when they grow up. Books about particular occupations allow kids to pretend to have that job for a little while.

Lastly, singing allows kids to hear words at a different tempo than they hear them in conversation. An added benefit is the repetition inherent in songs, which boosts understanding and memory. Create your own versions of common songs based on nonfiction information. You'll find a few examples in the text of this book.

Helpful Tips to Keep in Mind

The following are some tips on nonfiction books for preschoolers and ways to use them to create a successful movement-filled storytime.

- Some books will require more time when you add movement. This may mean that a storytime will have three books instead of four or five. Remember that the key is a positive and meaningful interaction with a book. It is okay if some books take longer than you are accustomed to.
- You do not have to make a big production out of every book. Some books will work best with very simple or minimal movements. Remember that what seems basic to adults may be a completely new experience for a child.
- Add the amount of movement that you think works best with a particular book and for your group. This means that some books will have movement on every page. It also means that some books will involve movement on only one or two pages. Do what feels natural, but also be flexible on the day of the program. I have had plans for particular movements with a book and then had participants spontaneously create another idea for the book. It's a great learning experience for everyone involved.
- Read the amount of text that makes sense for the kids in your storytime. Choose that amount based on the ages and interest level of your kids. You do not need to read every single word of text in a nonfiction book. Many nonfiction books for children offer general information in a large font and detailed information in a smaller font. Read just the large font

when sharing the book with a large crowd. The detailed information can be enjoyed later by a parent and child who are excited about the topic. For books that don't provide the ease of multiple font sizes, mark interesting sentences to be read with a Post-it note.

- Use different voices or inflection as you read a nonfiction book in storytime. Kids are already interested in learning about frogs, but it can be much more fun to say "ribbit" like a croaking frog than to read it like basic text.

- Be sure to model movements, activities, and art projects whenever possible. Preschool children are often looking for guidance in how to interact with the books. However, keep in mind that there are times when it can be fun to say "Act like a lion" and see what the kids come up with. The action suggestions in this book provide both instructions for activities and prompts for you to use with participants (including caregivers and yourself).

- Try to get the adults involved in the action too. There are many reasons why this is important. One, it helps strengthen the bond between a parent and a child. Two, parents can assist younger preschoolers who may have difficulty with some of the movements, especially when working with crayons. Three, it is always best to learn something by doing it. Once a parent has danced along with a book, he may think to repeat that action with another book at home.

- Be ready to adjust activities based on your storytime group. There will be days when everyone will calmly cooperate with movement. There will be days that it seems like an entire troop of monkeys has replaced your storytime crowd. Add more structure (like moving for a count of three, then finding stillness before moving to the next page) to keep everyone on track. Or let storytime run wild! It's really up to you.

- Keep in mind that the success of a movement or book may simply be related to the temperament of the storytime crowd that particular day. I have done back-to-back storytimes where a book was a huge hit in the first storytime and a huge failure in the second. If you really like an idea and it does not work the first time, try again another day.

- After storytime, take notes about the types of movement and activities that worked best with your group. Look for other ways to use those same types of movements with other books.

- If possible, put out extra copies of all the books read in storytime so that families can check out their favorites. Consider including other books on the same nonfiction topic, even some on a higher reading level. You have already sparked their interest in the topic, and families may wish to delve deeper into the information with an excited child.

- You may already be reading nonfiction to your storytime without realizing it. Many libraries catalog some nonfiction books with their picture books because they believe the particular books will be found by families better in that section. Take a quick glance at the Library of Congress cataloging information on the copyright page. Does it say "fiction" or "literature?" (For example, "dogs—fiction" or "dogs—literature") If it says "literature," it is a nonfiction title.

- Don't forget about nonfiction beginning-to-read titles. Many of them have clear, fun photographs or illustrations and a simple text. Reading these books in storytime is a great introduction to a potential reading source for a new reader.

- Some "simple" nonfiction books are much more than they seem. A simple counting book may also be providing information about the traits or routines of an animal. A great example of this is *One Wolf Howls* by Scotti Cohn. It counts from 1 to 12, it includes the months of the year, and it gives information about what wolves typically do during each month.

- If your budget allows funds for props, consider purchasing juggling scarves for storytime. They are extremely versatile in what they can represent in storytime—a blanket, a dog's tail, a hat, the blades of a helicopter, or a leaf falling from a tree. You will notice many ideas for using juggling scarves throughout this book.

- Use books that you like. This applies to any books that you choose for storytime whether they be fiction or nonfiction.

- Remember that storytime is all about fun. Kids who learn to love books will become good readers. The love of reading is a central building block for lifelong literacy.

chapter one

animals

Alinsky, Shelby. _Sleep, Bear!_

Washington, DC: National Geographic, 2015.

Summary: The bear is very hungry when he wakes up from his winter hibernation. Travel with him through spring, summer, and fall as he eats and eats and eats.

Action: Act out the book with the bear:

- Stretch as if you have just woken up from a long nap.
- Pretend to eat berries. Wipe the berry juice off your face.
- Pretend to eat bugs. Ewww!
- Pretend to eat grass.
- Pretend to eat more bugs and more grass.
- Pretend to eat a slippery, wiggly fish.
- Curl back down to hibernate again.

Action: Give everyone plastic toy bugs before beginning the book. Keep a bear puppet or stuffed animal with you while you read. Whenever the bear eats bugs, ask the kids to come up and feed your bear. If you are using a puppet, you can pretend to eat the bugs out of their hands.

Alinsky, Shelby. *Slither, Snake!*

Washington, DC: National Geographic, 2015.

Summary: This "pre-reader" beginning-to-read book introduces kids to eyelash tree vipers, western diamondback rattlesnakes, Arizona mountain king snakes, king cobras, sedge vipers, and boa constrictors. The text is quite simple, with captions naming the species of snake.

Action: The words "Slither, snake!" appear multiple times in the text. Slither along with the snakes by standing with your feet together and your arms down by your sides. Then wiggle your body like a snake.

Action: Add a prop to this book by giving everyone a juggling scarf or piece of ribbon or yarn that they can pretend is a snake. Have them slither/wiggle it on the floor along with the book.

Arndt, Ingo. *Best Foot Forward: Exploring Feet, Flippers, and Claws.*

New York: Holiday House, 2013.

Summary: Can you figure out the animal based on a picture of its foot? Play the guessing game, then learn a little about the animal.

Action: As you read about each animal in the book, pretend to walk like that animal.

- Try walking on all fours like a tiger.
- Pretend to climb high up in a tree like a gecko.
- Waddle like a duck.
- Move slowly like a tortoise.
- Bounce like a kangaroo.
- Snap your claws like a lobster.

Action: Add a little fun to the suspense of figuring out each animal. As you turn the page to reveal the animal, ask everyone to create a drumroll by slapping their hands on the floor.

Bader, Bonnie. *Pup-Pup-Puppies.*

New York: Penguin Young Readers, 2014.

Summary: This beginning-to-read book shows different types of puppies and gives very basic information about how to care for one.

Action: You'll find the words "puppy" and "puppies" multiple times in this book. Encourage everyone to bark or to hold up a die-cut dog every time they hear one of those words.

Action: Give everyone a die-cut dog at the end of the book so they can take it for a walk.

Baines, Becky. *A Den Is a Bed for a Bear: A Book about Hibernation.*
Washington, DC: National Geographic, 2008.

Summary: Where do bears sleep? And for how long? The combination of photographs and line drawings gives this title a scrapbook feel. The small trim size will make this book attractive to kids who want to look through it on their own after seeing it in storytime.

Action: Give every child a juggling scarf or other piece of fabric. They can pretend that the scarf is a blanket and curl up in their "den" for the first part of the book. When you get to the page when "winter is over," throw off the blankets to simulate leaving the den.

Action: Ask everyone to bring in their favorite stuffed bear (or give everyone a piece of felt in the shape of a bear). Place a large box at the front of the room and ask everyone to place their bear in the "cave" to hibernate. You may wish to place a blanket over the opening or close the box to make it dark and cozy for the bears. When "winter is over," pause so everyone can retrieve their bear from the cave.

Barner, Bob. *Animal Baths.*
San Francisco: Chronicle Books, 2011.

Summary: Monkeys groom their hair and pigs wallow in mud. But did you know that shrimp clean an eel's teeth? Barner's classic illustrations add lots of color to information about how animals bathe.

Action: Give everyone a juggling scarf or piece of fabric that they can pretend is a washcloth (or other cleaning instrument) throughout the book:

- Monkey: Rub the scarf on your hair.
- Elephant: Pretend the scarf is your trunk and spray water on your ears.
- Duck: Flap the scarf like wet feathers you are trying to dry off.
- Eel: Pretend to use the scarf to clean your teeth. (Ask the kids to not put the scarves in their mouths. However, you may still want to wash the scarves after this storytime.)
- Pig: Lay the scarf on the ground. Pretend it is mud and roll around on it.

- Manatee: Hold the scarf in your hand and have it "swim" toward you like a fish.
- Bat: Hold the scarf upside down as if it is a bat.
- Bear: Try to rub your back with the scarf.
- Shark: Pretend the scarf is a fish again and have it pick pretend dirt off of your body.
- Giraffe: Hold the scarf in the middle and flap the ends up and down like a bird's wings. Have it gently fly toward your neck.
- Person: Rub the scarf all over your body to get clean.

Barner, Bob. *Bears! Bears! Bears!*

San Francisco: Chronicle Books, 2010.

Summary: Learn about the eight species of bears through one sentence each. The simplicity of this book makes it ideal for the youngest preschooler.

Action: There is something very satisfying about growling at the top of your lungs. Encourage everyone to "*Grrr!*" like a bear at the end of each page.

Action: Teach everyone the sign for "bear" in American Sign Language. (Signing Savvy, www.signingsavvy.com, is a wonderful resource for learning specific signs.) Ask everyone to do the sign every time you say "bear" or "bears." Listen carefully; there is only one page where neither word appears.

Barton, Bethany. *I'm Trying to Love Spiders.*

New York: Viking, 2015.

Summary: A hilarious look at spiders and all the cool things they can do. Unfortunately, the narrator is also terrified of spiders and can't seem to stop squishing them. When a swarm of bugs takes over the book, the narrator finally accepts that spiders are good. Cockroaches, however, are a different story.

Action: Give everyone a die-cut spider before beginning the book. Whenever the narrator squishes the spider in the book, squish the spider in front of you. The narrator always seems to use her hand to splat the spider; for extra silliness, you can try using other body parts, such as your foot, elbow, or stomach.

Bedford, David. *Tails.*

Illus. Leonie Worthington. Prahan, Australia: Little Hare Books, 2007.

Summary: What kinds of animals have tails, and how do they use them? Written like a storybook, the trim size is small, but the illustrations are large and have fun flaps.

Action: Give everyone a juggling scarf or piece of thick ribbon that they can pretend is their tail. Play along with the book:

- Snake: Scrunch your tail up in a mess.
- Cat: Wrap your tail around yourself like a mother cat wrapping her tail around her kittens.
- Horse: Swish the tail back and forth.
- Skunk: Hold both ends of your tail so it stands up straight.
- Peacock: Hold the tail out wide (this works best with a juggling scarf).
- Monkey: Wrap your hand around your scarf as if your hand is a small monkey going for a ride.
- Dog: Flip your tail around and around.

Action: For a more simple way to interact with this book, give everyone a juggling scarf or ribbon and encourage them to tuck it into the back of their pants or tie it to a belt loop. Can they wag their tail after every page?

Berkes, Marianne. *Over in the Jungle: A Rainforest Rhyme.*

Illus. Jeanette Canyon. Nevada City, CA: Dawn Publications, 2007.

Summary: Learn the numbers 1 through 10 while discovering some less common rain forest animals. The polymer clay aspect of the illustrations adds depth and interest. The book can be sung to the tune of "Over in the Meadow."

Action: Count together at the end of each page. Clap or play an instrument as you count up to the correct number. This may seem repetitive to you, but you are helping little minds learn their numbers.

Action: On each page, the parent instructs the baby animals to swing, flit, squawk, scurry, scramble, squeeze, hop, pounce, creep, or hoot. Do these motions along with the animals. If you wish to continue the counting instruction, you can pretend to swing once, flit twice, squawk three times, and so on.

Bleiman, Andrew, and Chris Eastland. *ZooBorns! Zoo Babies from around the World.*

New York: Beach Lane Books, 2010.

Summary: Who can resist photographs of newborn animals? Common animals like the Asian elephant and uncommon animals like the crowned sifaka are featured alongside brief information.

Action: After reading each page, take a couple seconds to pretend to be each animal:

- Asian elephant: Hold your arm up to your nose to pretend you have a long trunk, or pretend to roll around a huge ball with your trunk.
- Fennec fox: Make huge ears with your hands and hold them up to your head.
- Sumatran orangutan: Spread your fingers wide and hold your hands up behind your head as if you have a head of bright hair sticking straight up.
- Tawny frogmouth: Open your mouth wide, really wide.
- Spotted hyena: Laugh like a hyena.
- Aardvark: Lightly pinch the skin on your cheeks to make wrinkles like this baby.
- Ocelot: Show your teeth.
- Gorilla: Open your eyes wide like the gorilla in this photo.
- Bengal tiger: Use your fingers to give yourself whiskers coming out of your cheeks.
- Kangaroo: Wiggle and snuggle into a comfy blanket.
- Banded mongoose: Mongooses mainly eat insects—pretend to eat one.
- Crowned sifaka: Hug a huge stuffed teddy bear.
- Pygmy hippo: Pretend to eat your greens.
- Wombat: Dig in the dirt.
- Okapi: Stick out your blue tongue.
- Anteater: Come up with a name for this little guy.
- Beluga whale: Pretend to swim in the ocean. Don't forget to smile.

Chrustowski, Rick. *Bee Dance.*

New York: Henry Holt, 2015.

> **Summary:** When a honeybee finds a field in bloom, she returns to the hive to tell the others. Her method of communication is a dance that tells the others where to go. This informational picture book reads like a story.

> **Action:** The honeybee's dance involves twirling and wagging her body. Dance along with the honeybee on the dancing pages.

> **Action:** After reading the two pages with the dancing honeybee, pause reading to play "The Flight of the Bumblebee." Encourage everyone to dance to the music.

> **Action:** Give everyone a fake flower and a straw so they can pretend to sip the nectar with their "bendy-straw tongue."

Cohn, Scotti. *One Wolf Howls.*

Illus. Susan Detwiler. Mt. Pleasant, SC: Sylvan Dell, 2009.

> **Summary:** How do wolves act throughout the year? Start in January and end in December, counting wolves from 1 to 12 along the way.

> **Action:** Focus on the movements/actions of the wolves on each page. Can you pretend you are part of their pack?

- January: Toss back your head and howl at the moon.
- February: Jump around and pretend to bat at another wolf that you are playing with. (Caution the children to be careful of their neighbors while they do this.)
- March: Do you see the humans? Give a warning bark.
- April: Keep your eyes wide open as you sniff the air for possible prey.
- May: Make yourself small like a newborn pup.
- June: Curl up in the warm sunshine.
- July: Trot through the grass. Wolves walk on all fours but you can walk on two feet to make it easier.
- August: Dance in the twilight.
- September: Hide behind your hands so no one can see you.
- October: Sniff at the ground.
- November: Curl up to stay warm in the snow.
- December: Howl and sing once more.

De La Bédoyère, Camilla, and Fiona Hajée. *Guess Who's . . . Furry.*
Irvine, CA: QEB Publishing, 2014.

———. ***Guess Who's in the Grass.***
Irvine, CA: QEB Publishing, 2014.

———. ***Guess Who's in the Sand.***
Irvine, CA: QEB Publishing, 2014.

———. ***Guess Who's in the Snow.***
Irvine, CA: QEB Publishing, 2014.

———. ***Guess Who's in the Trees.***
Irvine, CA: QEB Publishing, 2014.

———. ***Guess Who's . . . Noisy.***
Irvine, CA: QEB Publishing, 2014.

———. ***Guess Who's . . . Scary.***
Irvine, CA: QEB Publishing, 2014.

———. ***Guess Who's . . . Speedy.***
Irvine, CA: QEB Publishing, 2014.

Summary: Read the three questions, then lift the flap to reveal the animal. A small part of each animal peeks out from behind the flap, giving another clue to readers.

Action: Each page features three "who" questions and an enthusiastic "I do!" once the flap is raised. Encourage everyone to put their palms face up for each "who" question, then to point at themselves and yell "I do!" as the animal is revealed.

Action: Give everyone a couple pieces of long plastic grass for *Guess Who's in the Grass*. Hide behind the grass as the three questions are asked, then pop out, exclaiming, "I do!" like a game of peekaboo.

Action: Give everyone a scarf, hat, or mittens before reading *Guess Who's in the Snow*. Tell everyone that the animals in the book are well suited for the environment, but we aren't—without a little help. Add to the thought of cold by shivering with every page. You can also distribute cotton balls as little snowballs to add to the atmosphere.

Action: Give everyone a plastic leaf or die-cut leaf for *Guess Who's in the Trees*. Hide behind the leaf as the three questions are asked, then pop out, exclaiming, "I do!" like a game of peekaboo.

Action: While it can be done with any of the books, *Guess Who's . . . Noisy* is best for making the animal noises after each animal is revealed.

Action: Ask everyone to make scary faces while reading *Guess Who's . . . Scary*? Make a mean, scary face while acting like a brown bear, vulture, mako shark, tarantula spider, rattlesnake, and crocodile.

Action: How fast are the animals in *Guess Who's . . . Speedy*? After each animal is revealed, run in place to show how fast each animal moves. Is the antelope as fast as the cheetah?

Dunn, Mary R. *Fireflies.*

Mankato, MN: Capstone, 2012.

Summary: Many kids like to catch fireflies on warm summer evenings. This book shows photographs and gives a bit of information about these seemingly magic bugs.

Action: Put yellow dot stickers on the palms of kids before reading the book. At the end of each page, they can pretend that their hands are fireflies by opening and closing their fists. This activity can also be done without the stickers.

Action: Use a website like Oriental Trading (www.orientaltrading.com) to purchase a large number of cheap, small flashlights. (If you use a marketing company, you may be able to get a bunch of flashlights with your library name or logo on them.) Give a flashlight to everyone so they can make their own fireflies in the room. After you finish reading the book, turn off the lights so that the flashlight fireflies are easier to see.

Esbaum, Jill. *Animal Groups.*

Photo. Frans Lanting. Washington, DC: National Geographic, 2015.

Summary: Most people have heard of a litter of kittens or a herd of cattle. What about a celebration of polar bears or a cackle of hyenas? Learn about ten unique names for groups of animals alongside double-page photographs of each group.

Action: Can you act like each group of animals?

- Run fast like a cheetah.
- Walk on all fours like a polar bear.
- Make a beak with your hands to pretend you are an Atlantic puffin.
- Pretend to float in the water like a sea otter.
- Whinny like a zebra.
- Pretend to fly like a monarch butterfly.
- Laugh like a hyena.
- Pretend to jump from branch to branch like a monkey.
- Squawk like a macaw.
- Stretch your neck like a giraffe.

FitzSimmons, David. *Curious Critters.*
Bellville, OH: Wild Iris, 2011.

———. *Curious Critters Marine.*
Bellville, OH: Wild Iris, 2015.

———. *Curious Critters: Volume 2.*
Bellville, OH: Wild Iris, 2014.

Summary: Unique animals tell their first-person stories, sometimes in poetry, sometimes in lyrical language, and sometimes in song. Each quick story is complemented with a stunning photograph of the animal.

Action: The first volume features a spotted salamander with a story to the tune of "Rain, Rain, Go Away." Use a spray bottle to create rain in storytime while reading this page.

Action: Midway through the *Marine* book is the cushion sea star, whose story can be sung to the tune of "Twinkle, Twinkle, Little Star." Sing the song while everyone stands with their arms and legs out wide like a starfish. You can make the movement dynamic by swaying back and forth and lifting one foot and then the other.

Action: A couple pages into *Volume 2* is the predaceous diving beetle. Sing its story to the tune of "Row, Row, Row Your Boat" while acting it out: row your legs to pretend to swim, dive down into the water, and lastly, pretend to fly.

Action: Pick another animal that you like from the books and discover a way to imitate it while reading its story. Favorites in the first volume include:

- American bullfrog: Pretend to splash into water with it.
- Ohio crawfish: Make your hands look like claws and snap them together to warn animals to stay away.
- Southern flying squirrel: Spread out your arms and pretend to glide through the air.
- Jumping spider: Jump up high with it every time it jumps (thwip!).

Frattini, Stéphane. *Who's Looking at You?*
New York: Sterling Children's Books, 2012.

> **Summary:** Can you identify the animal based on a close-up photograph of its eye? Lift the flap to see if you are correct and learn a little about the animal. You will most likely want to leave the additional information for interested families to read later; many kids will want to rush to the next guess.

> **Action:** Give everyone a pair of paper binoculars to use. Tape two empty toilet paper rolls together, or create toilet paper rolls by using cardstock. If you wish, punch two holes in one end to add a yarn lanyard to the "binoculars." Encourage the kids to look through the binoculars to view the book. Can they guess each animal?

> **Action:** Does the animal on each page make a sound? Ask storytime participants to try to make the correct sound before the flap is lifted.

> **Action:** If you have parents and caregivers in your storytime, include them when reading this book. Ask them to cover their faces with their hands, revealing only one eye. Have the kids go to their adult to see how different she looks when showing only an eye.

Frisch, Aaron. *Butterflies.*
Mankato, MN: Creative Paperbacks, 2015.

> **Summary:** Very simple information about butterflies is provided, with minimal text and large, clear photographs.

> **Action:** Give everyone a white paper plate and some crayons before you start reading the book. Ask everyone to draw a flower on their paper plate while you read about butterflies. Read the book slowly so that kids can look at the photographs and work on their flowers. When you get to page 16, pull out a butterfly puppet or die-cut shape and fly to each flower drawn by the children.

Action: As an alternative to the last activity, give every child a die-cut butterfly shape. Spread fake flowers throughout your storytime space and let everyone fly among the flowers.

Action: Use this book as your storytime farewell. Give everyone a die-cut butterfly to play with while you read the book. The very last page reads, "Goodbye, butterflies!" Tell everyone that their butterflies are ready to fly out of the room and that they should help them.

Frisch, Aaron. *Frogs.*

Mankato, MN: Creative Paperbacks, 2015.

Summary: A simple introduction to frogs, including where they live, what they look like, and what they eat.

Action: If your library allows food, give every child a gummy worm to eat after reading pages 12–13, which talk about frogs eating bugs and worms.

Action: Frogs have very wide mouths. Give everyone a paper plate that has been folded in half. Instead of feeding gummy worms to the kids (previous activity), give everyone die-cut worms or insects to feed to their paper-plate frog mouth. You can also use pieces of yarn cut to worm length.

Action: Frogs often use their long tongues to catch food. Give everyone a noisemaker (the kind that is rolled up and shoots out straight when you blow it). Kids can pretend to be a frog with a long tongue.

Action: Hop and ribbit or croak at the end of every page.

Frisch, Aaron. *Ladybugs.*

Mankato, MN: Creative Paperbacks, 2015.

Summary: Very simple information about ladybugs is provided, with minimal text and large, clear photographs.

Action: Hide a bunch of ladybugs in your storytime space before reading the book. You can use die-cut shapes or paper plates with spots on them. On page 7, readers learn that ladybugs are sometimes found inside houses. Ask your group if they think ladybugs can get into the library. Pause the book and let everyone search for the ladybugs in your storytime space (like an egg hunt). Continue reading once all the ladybugs have been found.

Action: How many spots? On page 9, readers learn that ladybugs have black or white spots on their shells. Pause after reading this to share premade ladybug shells (paper plates with round black stickers or drawn black spots). Count the number of spots together.

Gray, Rita. *Have You Heard the Nesting Bird?*

Illus. Kenard Pak. Boston: Houghton Mifflin Harcourt, 2014.

Summary: All the birds are out making noise, except for one that sits quietly on her nest. At last we hear a tap and a crack and learn that she has been sitting on her eggs.

Action: Before beginning the book, give everyone a plastic egg to carefully hold in their hands. They can cup their hands to make them into a nest. During the story, when the eggs in the nest crack open, have everyone open up their plastic eggs. Make the activity more fun by putting a small pom-pom with googly eyes inside each egg.

Ham, Catherine. *Animal Naps.*

Waynesville, NC: EarlyLight Books, 2011.

Summary: Poetry matches with photographs of sleeping animals—sometimes informational, sometimes just fun.

Action: Ask the group if they could sleep like the animals in this book. Focus just on the photographs and try to mimic the way the animals are sleeping. Lie on your side like a kangaroo and put your paw over your face. Drape yourself around a few branches in a tree like a koala bear or red panda. Stand on one leg like a flamingo or a duck.

Ham, Catherine. *Open Wide! A Look inside Animal Mouths.*

Waynesville, NC: EarlyLight Books, 2012.

Summary: Photographs of a variety of animals with their mouths open wide accompany facts told through playful verse.

Action: Pick a few favorite pages to share with a storytime crowd. Encourage everyone to act like the animal on those pages. Examples include:

- Stand on your "hind legs" while looking about like a prairie dog.
- Hop around like a frog.
- Bend at your waist so you are looking upside down like a bat.
- Waddle like a penguin.

Action: Give everyone a copy of the mouth outline from the appendix and some crayons. Ask everyone to draw an animal to go along with the open mouth.

Action: Castanets can look like a mouth opening and closing; they also require dexterous fingers. Give everyone a pair of cheap castanets to play with while you share the book. You may choose to read some of the pages, or just show the fun photographs while reading the type of animal aloud. Encourage everyone to clap the castanet "mouths" together for each page.

Hansen, Grace. *Elephants.*
Minneapolis: Abdo Kids, 2016.

Summary: Photographs of these huge animals utilize two-thirds of each double-page spread. The rest is filled with minimal text surrounded by plentiful white space.

Action: Get ready for a noisy storytime. Give everyone a party noisemaker (found at any party supply store). At the end of each page, create your own herd of elephants by encouraging everyone to blow their noisemakers for a count of three.

Action: The elephants are spraying water in the photographs on two of the double-page spreads. Have a spray bottle of water ready and mist your storytime crowd on those two pages.

Action: Extend this story after reading by giving everyone elephant feet. Explain that elephants have very large feet, then tape paper plates to the bottoms of everyone's feet. Ask if it is more difficult to walk with such large feet.

Howard, Fran. *Bumble Bees.*
Mankato, MN: Capstone, 2005.

Summary: Learn about bumblebees as you look at pictures of them flying from flower to flower.

Action: Give everyone a fake flower before you start reading the book. Tell everyone to pretend that their finger is a bumblebee. They should pay close attention to the photograph on each page. If the bumblebee in the picture is on a flower, they should buzz their "finger bee" to their flower. If the bee in the picture in not on a flower, they should fly their "finger bee" around in the air.

Action: You can also do the previous activity using a yellow pom-pom to signify a bumblebee instead of using your finger. Put the pom-pom on the flower when it matches the picture. Fly the pom-pom around in the air when the bee is not on the flower. At the end of storytime, have everyone throw all the pom-poms up into the air to make it look like a swarm of bumblebees flying in your storytime.

Hulbert, Laura. *Who Has These Feet?*

Illus. Erik Brooks. New York: Henry Holt, 2011.

Summary: Can you guess the animal just by seeing its feet? Turn the page to see if you are correct and find out why each animal has those feet.

Action: Each of the animals has a very particular type of feet. Ask everyone to act like each animal in the book:

- Polar bear: Walk on all fours.
- Tree frog: Pretend the bottoms of your feet are sticky. Is it difficult to pull your feet up off of the floor?
- Duck: Waddle.
- Ant: Pretend to dig in the ground.
- Squirrel: Pretend to run up a tree.
- Parrot: Use your hands to hold on to a pretend branch.
- Desert lizard: Run across the hot sand. Hot! Hot! Hot!
- Sea turtle: Hold your hands out like flippers and pretend to swim through the water.
- Kangaroo: Jump.

Hulbert, Laura. *Who Has This Tail?*

Illus. Erik Brooks. New York: Henry Holt, 2012.

Summary: Can you guess the animal just by seeing an illustration of its tail? Turn the page to see the animal and find out how they use their tail.

Action: Give everyone a juggling scarf or piece of thick ribbon to act as a tail. Pretend to use the tail the same way the animals in the book use theirs:

- Monkey: Hold one arm out straight and loop the tail over it, as if your arm is a branch.
- Rattlesnake: Shake the tail and make a rattling noise.

- Shark: Flip the tail back and forth like a shark is swimming.
- Gerbil: A gerbil uses its tail to help it balance. People don't need help from a tail, but you can balance on one leg to play along.
- Horse: Use the tail to flick imaginary flies off of your back.
- Scorpion: Pretend to sting your leg with the tail.
- Peacock: Hold the tail out wide and show everyone how pretty it is.
- Arctic fox: Wrap the tail around you to stay warm.
- Beaver: Use the tail like a steering wheel.

Hurley, Jorey. *Nest.*

New York: Simon & Schuster Books for Young Readers, 2014.

Summary: Using only one word per page, this book shows readers the life cycle of a robin as an egg is laid, the hatchling learns to fly, and finally it meets a mate and they make a nest. Everything happens over the course of a year.

Action: Give kids a copy of the tree outline from the appendix and a crayon. As you read the book, they can add a bird's nest to the tree.

Action: Give kids a copy of the bird outline from the appendix and a crayon. As you read the book, they can draw a nest around the bird.

Jenkins, Steve, and Robin Page. *How to Swallow a Pig.*

Boston: Houghton Mifflin Harcourt, 2015.

Summary: Have you ever wondered how to catch fish like a humpback whale does, or how to build a nest like a wasp? With this book set up like an instruction manual, readers can learn how to do these and more in a few quick steps.

Action: Pick a couple of your favorite pages to act out with a storytime crowd. Pages that will work especially well are "Trap Fish Like a Humpback Whale," "Repel Insects Like a Capuchin," "Crack a Nut Like a Crow," "Catch a Meal Like a Crocodile," and "Defend Yourself Like an Armadillo." Don't forget to leave out copies of the book for families that want to learn how to act like all the animals in the book.

Jenkins, Steve, and Robin Page. *Move!*

Boston: Houghton Mifflin, 2006.

Summary: Animals walk, swim, climb, and fly. Find out how common animals (such as the blue whale and the crocodile) and less common animals (such as the jacana and the roadrunner) move. Each animal is illustrated through cut and torn paper collage that stands out against a white background.

Action: The title of this book instructs everyone to move along with the story. Pretend to swing, walk, dive, swim, leap, slither, climb, fly, run, dance, float, slide, and waddle along with the animals.

Action: Play lively, wordless music to accompany each movement. The kids can "dance" the movement for a few seconds before you turn the music off and start the next page. Using the music is a great way to notify kids that it is time to stop moving without you having to say "Stop!"

Kennard, Pippa. *Bunny Island*.
Photo. Yukihiro Fukuda. Buffalo, NY: Firefly Books, 2015.

Summary: Travel to Okunoshima Island to play with the wild bunnies. Many action words accompany the photographs of these playful creatures.

Action: Ask everyone to hop like a bunny and wiggle their nose at the end of every page.

Action: Pretend to follow along with the action words on each page: "zoom" *(run quick)*, "hop," "dig," "drip" *(pretend to shake water off like you were just swimming)*, "ha ha" *(laugh)*, "wiggle," "munch" *(pretend to eat something)*, "slurp" *(pretend to drink water)*, "yawn," "lick" *(pretend to lick your paws)*, "kiss," "zzz" *(lay down for sleep)*.

Action: You can add an extension activity to this book by doing the bunny hop with kids after you have finished reading.

Komiya, Teruyuki. *Life-Size Zoo*.
Photo. Toyofumi Fukuda. New York: Seven Footer Kids, 2009.

Summary: The oversize pages still can't contain the life-size photographs of animals, from a panda to an elephant to a koala. Share the short amount of text or just gaze at the stunning photography.

Action: How do these animals act? Can you make a movement like the animals in the book? Perhaps you can trot like a zebra, stick your tongue out like a giraffe, or pretend to climb a tree like a koala. Have the participants do movements for each animal, or just pause on the pages that make the most sense to you.

Action: The life-size photographs give you a basic idea of how large (or small) each animal is. Try to make your body the same size as each animal. It will be impossible to truly get as large as an elephant, but maybe you can squish as small as a koala.

London, Jonathan. *Hippos Are Huge!*

Illus. Matthew Trueman. Somerville, MA: Candlewick, 2015.

Summary: They may look docile and squishy, but these huge animals are the most dangerous animals in Africa. The illustrations show varying perspectives, from a mouth that looks like it is ready to chomp down on the reader to the stinky backsides. Full of interesting facts about these creatures, the book does not shy away from delicate subjects; older preschoolers will love seeing the hippo chomp down on a crocodile.

Action: Did I mention that "hippos are huge"? This is a fun phrase to add to the end of each page. Have everyone say it loud and proud while making their body as big as they can.

Action: Pay close attention to the illustrations. Is there a hippo on that page with its mouth wide open? If so, open up your arms as if they are a hippo's mouth ready to chomp. Close your arms together if all the hippos on the page have their mouths closed.

Lunis, Natalie. *Prickly Sea Stars.*

New York: Bearport, 2008.

Summary: Most people see only dried sea stars in a store by the beach. This book, filled with underwater photographs, gives a lot of information about these mysterious creatures. Depending on your audience, you may wish to read just some of the text on each page—perhaps the captions.

Action: Pages 16–17 talk about how sea stars can regrow rays that they lose. After reading those pages, have everyone hold an arm in tight to their body, then slowly move it back out like it is growing. You can also try doing this with a leg, but you might want to sit down first.

Action: Hold your arms and legs out wide so you can be a sea star throughout the book. You can have extra fun with a few of the pages:

- Pages 8–9: Use the ends of your hands to "look" around the room.
- Pages 10–11: Pretend to grab a huge clam or mussel with your arms and legs, then slowly pry it open.
- Pages 12–13: Stick your stomach out.

- Pages 14–15: Sea stars move slowly. Try to slowly get away from something that wants to eat you.
- Pages 16–17: Regrow a ray.

Markovics, Joyce. *Wood Frogs.*

New York: Bearport, 2015.

Summary: Did you know that frogs hibernate? In fact, they can freeze in place for days or weeks.

Action: Pretend to hibernate along with the frog. Hop once at the end of every page until the frog starts to hibernate (pages 8–9). Then get into a frog stance by bending your knees and putting your hands on the floor between your feet. Try to hold this position until the frog in the book moves again. (You can add to this action by putting a juggling scarf or piece of fabric on top of your head as if it is a leaf covering a frog.)

Action: Give everyone a die-cut frog and a die-cut leaf shape. When the frog rests under the leaf on pages 8–9, have everyone put their leaf over their frog. When the frog in the book moves again, remove the leaf and make the frog shape jump.

Neuman, Susan B. *Go, Cub!*

Washington, DC: National Geographic, 2014.

———. *Jump, Pup!*

Washington, DC: National Geographic, 2014.

Summary: These "pre-reader" beginning-to-read titles introduce readers to a young lion cub or puppy. The easy-to-read text is accompanied by large photographs of the animals.

Action: Pretend you are the lion cub or puppy and act out each page as it is read.

Neuman, Susan B. *Swim, Fish! Explore the Coral Reef.*

Washington, DC: National Geographic, 2014.

Summary: Underwater photographs take you up close with coral reef animals in this "pre-reader" beginning-to-read title. Captioned animals include clownfish, sergeant majors, seahorses, green sea turtles, giant moray eels, whale sharks, cushion sea stars, and minnows.

Action: Check your local dollar store for diving masks or swimming goggles. Give everyone a mask or goggles to wear while you read to simulate a snorkeling experience.

Action: Give everyone a plain piece of paper and some crayons. While you read the book, they can draw their own underwater world.

Action: Pretend to be each of the animals featured in the book:

- School of fish: Pretend your hand is a fish and make it quickly dart back and forth.
- Seahorse: Hold up one finger, giving it a slight bend to make it look like a seahorse body. Make your finger swim up, down, and sideways.
- Turtle: Hold all your fingers together like a flipper, hold your arms in close, and pretend to swim through the water.
- Eel: Wiggle your body like an eel.
- Whale shark: Open your mouth wide like a big whale shark.
- Sea star: Hold your arms and legs out wide, creating a star shape with your body. Slowly walk forward, keeping your legs spread wide.
- Minnow: Move around as quickly as you can.

Rake, Jody Sullivan. *Meerkats.*

Mankato, MN: Capstone, 2008.

Summary: Explore the African world of a meerkat. Photographs of these fascinating creatures span a majority of each two-page spread.

Action: Build imaginary burrows for all your meerkat participants. Use hula hoops or tape to designate the holes into their burrows. Ask everyone to stand guard by their holes, looking for danger ("Be sure to stand nice and tall as you look around.") Have everyone run and jump into the closest burrow on the last double-page spread to hide underground.

Riggs, Kate. *Brown Bears.*

Mankato, MN: Creative Education / Creative Paperbacks, 2015.

Summary: The stars of this book are the large, engaging photographs of brown bears. Read all the text or just the captions, or take a picture walk to enjoy this book with preschoolers.

Action: Ask everyone to pretend to do what the bears are doing on each page. Some prompts you may use include: "Can you stand in the same pose as the bear?," "Can you pretend to eat a fish?," and "Can you pretend to climb a tree?" Be careful on the fighting page that kids "fight with the air" and not each other.

Action: Hide a stuffed bear (or picture of a bear) somewhere in your story-time space before the program. If possible, hide it somewhere that you can pretend is a bear's den for hibernating. After reading page 15, where it says, "Bears spend the winter sleeping in dens," have everyone search for the sleeping bear. Continue the book after the bear is found. Be sure to remind everyone that they should never approach, touch, or bother a real bear that is hibernating.

Action: Bears like to rub their backs on trees (see pages 18 and 19). After reading this spread, have everyone move to a wall or other suitable spot to scratch their backs like a bear.

Riggs, Kate. *Eagles.*

Mankato, MN: Creative Paperbacks, 2015.

Summary: See close-up photographs of eagles as you learn about their bodies, where they live, and what they eat.

Action: Give everyone a fake feather or two so they can pretend to fly with the eagles. If possible, make sure the feathers are brown, black, gray, or white to match an eagle's feathers. Ask everyone to flap the feathers to "fly" whenever the eagle in the photograph is flying. On page 17, use your hands to "clean" the feather like the eagle in the picture (do not use your mouth/beak like the eagle in the photograph).

Riggs, Kate. *Flamingos.*

Mankato, MN: Creative Education / Creative Paperbacks, 2015.

Summary: Unless you live in the flamingos' natural habitat, this colorful bird can seem strange and exotic. Enjoy full-page photographs as you explore this tropical bird.

Action: Flamingos are often seen standing on one leg. Have everyone stand up and stand on one leg while you read the book. If they lose their balance, encourage them to try again. If this is too hard for a younger group, just have them stand on one leg while you read page 20, which features a flamingo standing on one leg.

Action: The tree pose in yoga resembles a flamingo standing on one leg. Use this book as an opportunity to introduce that pose to storytime participants.

Action: Page 11 states that flamingos "have to get a running start before flying." If you have space, ask everyone to practice running before flapping their arms to "fly."

Riggs, Kate. *Geckos.*

Mankato, MN: Creative Education / Creative Paperbacks, 2015.

Summary: Learn about the noisy and colorful gecko, even if you don't live in a warm climate.

Action: On page 7, the book tells us that geckos "lick their eyes to keep them clean." Pause and let everyone try to lick their own eye.

Action: Also on page 7, we learn that geckos can break off their tails to escape from an enemy. Give everyone a juggling scarf and have them hold it at the small of their back like a tail. Ask everyone to pair up to break away the tails from each other.

Action: On page 4, readers learn that geckos make a sound like a bark or a chirp. After reading that, play a video or sound clip of a gecko and ask everyone to try to mimic the sound. One possible video is this YouTube clip of a tokay gecko: https://www.youtube.com/watch?v=dR9tn0yNqQo.

Riggs, Kate. *Pandas.*

Mankato, MN: Creative Education / Creative Paperbacks, 2015.

Summary: Close-up photographs and short text introduce kids to these popular animals.

Action: Create a simple panda bear out of felt to put on your flannelboard. Give everyone a piece of felt in the shape of a long, thin green bamboo leaf. When you get to the page that talks about pandas eating bamboo, ask everyone to place their leaf on the flannelboard near the panda so it has something to eat. If you have a panda stuffed animal, you can do the same activity with green paper leaves.

Action: Pretend you are a panda while reading the book:

- Show your claws.
- Open your mouth wide to show all your teeth.
- Pretend to use those teeth to eat bamboo.
- Pretend to climb a tree.
- Lastly, fall asleep up in that tree. (This activity makes this book a great end to storytime because it calms everyone down.)

Riggs, Kate. *Sea Turtles.*

Mankato, MN: Creative Education / Creative Paperbacks, 2015.

Summary: Go underwater to explore sea turtles. The book features large photographs of these majestic animals.

Action: Give everyone a white paper plate and some crayons. Tell them to pretend that the back of the plate is a turtle's shell. They can color the shell however they like while you read the book.

Action: Sea turtles spend most of their time in the water, but they do come up on land occasionally. Look at the pictures on each page—is the turtle swimming in the water or crawling on the beach? Pretend to swim or crawl to represent what the turtles are doing on each page.

Riggs, Kate. *Sharks.*

Mankato, MN: Creative Paperbacks, 2014.

Summary: What is it about sharks that both frightens and fascinates us? Learn a few brief facts while looking at underwater photographs of these big fish.

Action: Sharks are known for their pointy teeth and strong jaws. Ask everyone to open their arms up wide (one up and one down) and "chomp" down after reading each page.

Action: While we think of sharks as something completely different, they really are just fish. Put your palms together in front of you and pretend your hands are a fish swimming through the water. If you stick your thumbs up, you'll add a fin to your shark.

Action: Give everyone a copy of the shark outline from the appendix and some crayons. Kids can either color their shark or create an underwater world around it while you read the book.

Riggs, Kate. *Snakes.*

Mankato, MN: Creative Paperbacks, 2014.

Summary: Photographs and minimal text give a brief introduction to snakes. Pages 12–13 feature a snake eating a mouse and a frog; you may want to consider your audience before sharing this spread.

Action: On page 9 it states, "They do not have arms or legs." Have everyone hold their arms down by their sides and wiggle their bodies like a snake for the rest of the book.

Action: Give everyone a two-foot-long piece of thick rope. (Yarn will also work; rope is recommended because it is thicker, like a snake.) Show the kids how to wiggle their "snake" and make it move along the ground while you read the book.

Action: Challenge everyone to enjoy the book while trying the snake (cobra) yoga pose. Ask them to lie on their stomach, then use their arms to push up their upper body. This activity will work best with a smaller group because kids in the back of a large group will not be able to see the book. If you normally sit on a chair during storytime, be sure to sit on the floor for this book so kids aren't straining their necks to look up. Encourage everyone to play around with the pose since most will not be able (or wish) to hold the pose for the whole book.

Rissman, Rebecca. *Ants.*

Chicago: Raintree, 2013.

Summary: Part of the Creepy Critters series. Readers learn about ants through large photographs, cartoon backgrounds, and rhyming text.

Action: There are three opportunities to count together in this book: count the body parts on pages 6–7, count the legs on pages 8–9, and count the ants on pages 22–23. Count aloud together and clap or stomp for each number.

Action: On pages 12–13, the reader learns that "ants like to march in line." Take a break from reading to march around the room to the song "The Ants Go Marching." Sing the words yourself or use this fun YouTube video: https://www.youtube.com/watch?v=Pjw2A3QU8Qg. Note that the video provides verses all the way up to marching ten by ten. Play the entire song (four minutes and ten seconds), or continue reading after a couple verses.

Rissman, Rebecca. *Beetles.*

Chicago: Raintree, 2013.

Summary: Part of the Creepy Critters series. Readers learn about beetles through large photographs, cartoon backgrounds, and rhyming text.

Action: Give everyone two large paper plates to use as wings. Have them hold one plate in each hand, then cross their arms over their body and hold the plates behind their shoulders to look like beetle wings folded on top of their body. Everyone flaps the wings on any pages that show a beetle flying; otherwise, they hold them still.

Rissman, Rebecca. *Caterpillars.*
Chicago: Raintree, 2013.

Summary: Before they become butterflies or moths, caterpillars have to find food and protect themselves from predators.

Action: Put about eight beads on a piece of yarn. Tie a large knot on each end so that the beads don't fall off. Give a bead "caterpillar" to each child to play with while you read the book. For extra fun, give everyone a die-cut leaf so their caterpillar has something to crawl on.

Rissman, Rebecca. *Dragonflies.*
Chicago: Raintree, 2013.

Summary: Part of the Creepy Critters series. Readers learn about dragonflies through large photographs, a cartoon background, and rhyming text.

Action: Dragonflies have large eyes (as you learn on page 6). Ask everyone, "How can you make your eyes look bigger?" Show participants how to make circles with their hands and hold them in front of their eyes. You can also give everyone two die-cuts of the letter "O" to hold in front of their eyes to make them look bigger. Enjoy the rest of the book with your extra-large eyes.

Action: Dragonflies have four wings. Give everyone four juggling scarves to flap in the wind like a dragonfly at the end of each page. You can also use four pieces of thick ribbon for this activity.

Rockwell, Lizzy. *A Bird Is a Bird.*
New York: Holiday House, 2015.

Summary: Birds come in all sizes and colors, but there are many ways that they are similar. Learn how they are alike and how they differ from all other animals. Each of the birds in the detailed illustrations is identified for inquisitive minds.

Action: Give everyone a copy of the bird outline from the appendix and a choice of crayon colors. As you read the book, everyone can color their bird however they wish. When you get to the last double-page spread, "Feathers of every color cover birds of every kind . . . ," have everyone hold up their colorful birds to mirror the variety of colors in the illustration.

Action: This title has many great words that kids can act out while you read. Have them stand tall, then get small. They can pretend to catch a fish or peck at wood with a beak. They can fly with two wings or curl up in a pretend egg. Take a few moments on each page to see what everyone can act out.

Rustad, Martha E. H. *Animals in Fall.*
Mankato, MN: Capstone, 2008.

Summary: It's time to start getting ready for winter. Find out how geese, monarch butterflies, snowshoe hares, deer, squirrels, honey bees, and bears spend the season preparing.

Action: Squirrels hide nuts that they can eat later. Once you have read that page, give everyone a small paper acorn or nut to hide somewhere in your storytime space. Once they have hidden their "food," they should come back for the rest of the book. If you do storytime on the general library floor, you may be finding acorns for months after reading this book. You may decide to make a game out of it by rewarding found acorns with a sticker or stamp.

Rustad, Martha E. H. *Animals in Winter.*
Mankato, MN: Capstone, 2009.

Summary: How do animals survive the winter? Some migrate. Some hibernate. Some forage for food. Briefly learn about a few animals in winter.

Action: Ask everyone to pretend to act like each animal in this book.

- Flap your wings to fly south with the geese.
- Dig under the snow with the reindeer.
- Go to sleep with the hibernating bear and bats.
- Swim very slowly at the bottom of the lake with the fish.
- Look for hidden nuts with the squirrel.
- Hop in the snow like the snowshoe hare.

Sayre, April Pulley. *Ant, Ant, Ant! (An Insect Chant).*
Illus. Trip Park. Minnetonka, MN: NorthWord Books for Young Readers, 2005.

————. *Bird, Bird, Bird! (A Chirping Chant).*

Illus. Gary Locke. Minnetonka, MN: NorthWord Books for Young Readers, 2007.

Summary: Readers are introduced to many North American insects, with the bug names featured alongside expressive illustrations. The names are arranged so that the entire book can be read to a rhythm. A few sentences about each insect can be found in the back. *Bird, Bird, Bird!* follows the same formula, introducing kids to birds that can be found in North America but may also migrate south.

Action: Get everyone clapping or shaking a maraca to a slow, easy beat. Read the book to the beat. For example, the first page of *Ant, Ant, Ant!* reads like this (clap with the capital letters): "BRUSH-footed BUT-TERfly, LEAF-footed BUG, BIRD dropping CATERpillar, SLUG, slug, SLUG." The first page of *Bird, Bird, Bird!* can be read like this: "WAN-Dering TATTler, TIMBERdoodle, TEAL. NUTcracker, GNATcatcher, ARE these REAL?" Be sure to practice reading these books a few times before sharing them in storytime.

Sayre, April Pulley. *Honk, Honk, Goose! Canada Geese Start a Family.*

Illus. Huy Voun Lee. New York: Henry Holt, 2009.

Summary: Watch as two geese form a family. The illustrations and active text follow the geese from courtship to mating to nest to chicks.

Action: The male goose spends a lot of time honking, hissing, and flapping his wings in order to protect the nest and his new family. Have everyone honk, hiss, and flap their arms along with him.

Sayre, April Pulley. *Woodpecker Wham!*

Illus. Steve Jenkins. New York: Henry Holt, 2015.

Summary: Follow along with a variety of woodpeckers as they peck away at a hole, hide from a hawk, and feed their young. Four rhyming lines of text on each page are quick and short, making for an easy storytime read.

Action: Give everyone a set of rhythm sticks before you start reading the book. At the end of each page, participants clap the sticks together to mimic a woodpecker's peck.

Action: The woodpeckers are not pecking on every page of the book. Ask everyone to listen carefully for instances when the woodpeckers chop, bonk, slam, tap, and wham. When they hear this, they should slap their hands on the ground to imitate the noise. This activity encourages strong listening skills in children.

Schuetz, Kari. *African Elephants.*

Minneapolis: Bellwether Media, 2012.

Summary: Part of the Blastoff! Readers series. Photographs of elephants are matched with easy-to-read text.

Action: It can be fun for the group to act like elephants together:

- Pages 4–5: Put your hands up to your ears to make it look like you have big, floppy elephant ears.
- Pages 6–7: Pretend your fingers are the end of an elephant's trunk and try to pinch leaves off of a tree.
- Pages 8–9: Use your whole arm like a trunk that is trying to pick up plants or something else to eat.
- Pages 10–11: Pretend your arms are tusks that are digging into the ground.
- Pages 12–13: Pretend to spray water on yourself using your arm as a trunk. (You may also want to use a spray bottle to spray participants with water.)
- Pages 14–15: Use your trunk to cover your body with dust. Don't forget to close your eyes.
- Pages 16–17: Walk like a big, heavy elephant.
- Pages 18–19: Throw your tusk up in the air and trumpet loudly.
- Pages 20–21: Give yourself (or a friend or family member) a hug.

Scott, Peter David, illus. *Amazing Animals.*

San Diego: Silver Dolphin, 2015.

Summary: Vivid illustrations and single sentences introduce kids to common (western gorilla) and not-so-common (flying fish) animals. A field guide in the back gives more information about each animal. The large trim size adds to the desire to look through this book again and again.

Action: Create a new version of "If You're Happy and You Know It" to go along with the book's title. Instead, sing "If You're Amazing and You

Know It" for each page or a collection of your favorite pages, using the lines from below for each animal. For example, with the western gorilla:

If you're amazing and you know it, beat your chest.
If you're amazing and you know it, beat your chest.
If you're amazing and you know it, your actions will surely show it.
If you're amazing and you know it, beat your chest.

- Western gorilla: . . . beat your chest.
- Birds of paradise: . . . show off like a bird. *(pretend you are in a fashion show and show off your feathers)*
- Golden poison dart frog: . . . sit like a frog. *(bend your knees and put your hands on the ground between your feet)*
- Sea horse: . . . carry your babies. *(hold your hands like you have a pouch near your chest)*
- Lionfish: . . . show your spines. *(hold your hands and fingers out wide)*
- Duck-billed platypus: . . . swim around. *(pretend to swim)*
- Three-toed sloth: . . . move very slowly.
- Emperor penguin: . . . hold an egg on your feet. *(pretend to stand very carefully)*
- Reticulated python: . . . be really long. *(stretch as tall as you can)*
- Panther chameleon: . . . change your colors. *(laugh and joke that people can't really do that)*
- Giant panda: . . . eat some bamboo.
- Beaver: . . . cut down a tree. *(pretend to gnaw on a tree stump)*
- Giant tortoise: . . . walk like a tortoise. *(walk on all fours)*
- Cheetah: . . . run really fast. *(run in place)*
- Fruit bat: . . . hang upside down. *(bend over at the waist to pretend to hang upside down)*
- Humpback whale: . . . sing to your friends.
- Ostrich: . . . show your long neck. *(stretch your neck tall)*
- Flying fish: . . . fly through the air. *(flap your "fins" as you fly)*
- Orangutan: . . . stretch your long arms. *(stretch out your arms wide or tall to show how long they are)*
- Hippopotamus: . . . open your mouth wide.

- Coelacanth: . . . swim like a fish.
- Colossal squid: . . . show your large eyes. *(make circles with your hands and hold them over your eyes, making them appear larger)*

Shingu, Susumu. *Traveling Butterflies.*
Berkeley, CA: Owlkids Books, 2015.

Summary: Written in storybook format, this is the tale of a monarch butterfly from when it hatches as a caterpillar to when it flies south to mate to when it ultimately returns home many months later.

Action: The butterfly spends a lot of time flying throughout the book. Encourage everyone to stand and flap their arms to "fly" along with the butterfly whenever she is flying.

Action: Expand upon the idea above by having everyone start curled up in a tiny ball (as if they are in the egg), pretending to crawl around munching on milkweed when she is still a caterpillar, then flying south.

Action: When the caterpillar wraps herself in a cocoon, give everyone a piece of fabric to wrap around themselves like a cocoon. When the new butterfly breaks out of her cocoon, everyone can pretend to do the same with the fabric.

Action: If you have the opportunity to read this story outside, choose a large open area such as a park. Start reading the book in one corner of the park. When the butterfly starts to fly south, slowly start "flying" toward another corner of the park. Once the butterfly arrives in the south, turn around to see how far your group has "flown." You can also do this activity in a large room.

Stewart, Melissa. *Feathers: Not Just for Flying.*
Illus. Sarah S. Brannen. Watertown, MA: Charlesbridge, 2014.

Summary: Illustrated to look like a field journal, this book demonstrates all the amazing things feathers can do besides helping a bird to fly. Read just the largest text to share this book with a storytime crowd.

Action: Give everyone a fake feather that they can interact with on many pages in the book. Model the interactions and/or use the following prompts to direct movement:

- Hold the feather close like a blanket.
- Lay your head on the feather as if it is a pillow.
- Hold the feather above your head like a sunshade.

- Use the feather like a washcloth to clean up messes.
- Hide behind your feather.
- Shake the feathers while making a whistling sound.
- Show everyone else your feather like you have some pretty jewelry.
- Use the feather like a shovel and dig a hole.
- Glide your feather across the floor like a sled.
- Flap your feather to fly.

Stockdale, Susan. *Bring On the Birds.*
Atlanta: Peachtree, 2011.

Summary: Birds can swoop, dance, hide, and drum. Simple rhyming text accompanies the bright and crisp illustrations of the birds. Each bird is identified in the back matter.

Action: The book uses many action-filled words throughout. Try to act out each page after you read it.

Action: Play the sounds/songs of some of the birds as you get to the corresponding page. Ask everyone to try to mimic the sound. Use a site such as eNature.com to easily search for many of the birds featured in this book (the search box is in the upper right corner).

Stockdale, Susan. *Carry Me! Animal Babies on the Move.*
Atlanta: Peachtree, 2005.

Summary: How do animal parents carry their young? Do their babies ride on their backs? Do they carry their babies in their mouths? This informative book reads like a soothing story.

Action: Ask everyone to bring their favorite stuffed animal to storytime, or give everyone a piece of felt in the shape of any animal featured in the book. As you read, encourage everyone to hold their baby like the animal on that page. They will hold their babies close to their bellies, on their feet, and nestled in their pretend feathers. On the last page, ask the kids to go snuggle with their parent like the human baby in the book.

Stockdale, Susan. *Fabulous Fishes.*
Atlanta: Peachtree, 2008.

Summary: Rhyming text and colorful illustrations introduce readers to fish of all shapes and sizes.

Action: Give everyone a die-cut fish before beginning the book. During most of the book they can simply make their fish pretend to swim. There are a few pages that they can do something special:

- They can hide the fish behind their hands on page 3.
- They can pretend their fish has pointy spikes—*ouch*—on page 5.
- They can pretend their fish is flying on pages 6–7.
- They can pretend their fish is walking on the ground on page 9.
- They can hold their fish up to their arm as if it is taking a ride on a really big fish on pages 18–19.
- They can lay their fish flat on the ground on page 20.

Action: Give everyone a copy of the fish outline from the appendix and some crayons. While you read the book, they can create their own fabulous fish.

Stockdale, Susan. *Stripes of All Types.*

Atlanta: Peachtree, 2013.

Summary: Who knew that stripes can be found so many places in nature? Rhyming text describes the places you can find all these differently striped animals.

Action: Animals have stripes in lots of different places: on their legs, on their wings, and sometimes on their whole body. Pause after reading each page for participants to draw imaginary stripes on their body to match the stripes on the animal in the illustration.

Action: Add a prop to the previous activity by giving everyone a clean paintbrush so they can pretend to paint stripes on themselves.

Action: At the end of the book, look for stripes in your storytime space. Is anyone wearing stripes? Do any other books have stripes? What about pictures on the wall? Or a pattern in the carpet?

Sweeney, Alyse. *Frogs.*

Mankato, MN: Capstone, 2010.

Summary: It seems like every kid wants to pick up frogs. This book teaches readers about their favorite amphibian.

Action: Show participants how to sit patiently like a frog throughout the book. Bend your knees and put your hands on the ground in between your feet. Encourage them to sit quietly just like the frogs in the book except on two pages. On page 10, jump up like the frog in the picture. On page 16, pretend your arm is a long, sticky tongue trying to catch a bug. At the end of book, hop around the room like a frog.

Action: Add more movement to the book by jumping like a frog at the end of every page. Don't forget to ribbit and croak.

Wadsworth, Ginger. *Up, Up, and Away.*

Illus. Patricia J. Wynne. Watertown, MA: Charlesbridge, 2009.

Summary: An action-packed account of a spider's life from egg to hatching to soaring above the sky in search of a new home, then to laying new eggs. While not all of the siblings survive, the watercolor illustrations tone down the reality of a spiderling's chances of survival.

Action: Give everyone a small piece of yarn that they can pretend is a spider's silken thread kite. When the main spider in the story takes off, everyone can throw their yarn up in the air to simulate a bunch of spiders taking off. If possible, turn on a fan to blow the yarn around the room.

Action: Rather than throwing the yarn up in the air, encourage children to roam around the room with their piece of yarn held high as they look for a suitable place for their spider to land.

Wahman, Wendy. *Don't Lick the Dog: Making Friends with Dogs.*

New York: Henry Holt, 2009.

Summary: Many small children want to interact with dogs. This is a child-friendly introduction to the best ways to treat a dog so that you can become friends.

Action: Ask everyone to bring a stuffed animal to storytime. If this is not feasible, give everyone a piece of felt in the shape of a dog (use your die-cut machine or ask volunteers to do the cutting) that they can interact with throughout the book. Be sure to model these good behaviors with your own stuffed animal:

- Ask the children to repeat after you as you ask an imaginary person if you may pet their dog. Tell everyone that the imaginary person has said yes and they may now carefully pet their own stuffed animal or felt dog.
- Curl your fingers under and let your pretend dog sniff your hand.
- Turn away from your dog when it wants to run and hide.

- Gently stroke your pretend dog's chin.
- Hold your hand like a plate and give pretend treats to your dog.
- Stand up straight and put your dog down on the ground, allowing it to walk away if it wishes.

Ward, Jennifer. *Mama Built a Little Nest.*

Illus. Steve Jenkins. New York: Beach Lane Books, 2014.

Summary: Birds build nests in trees, on ledges, and in the ground. They use interesting building supplies such as spiderwebs, floating twigs, and saliva. Four lines of rhyming text introduce children to these wondrous egg nurseries. Additional information is included on each page for those who want to know more.

Action: Give everyone a copy of the bird outline from the appendix and some crayons. While you read the book, kids can draw a nest and eggs around the bird. If you are super ambitious, put out leaves and small twigs that can be glued to the picture after storytime.

Action: Extend this book after reading it by going on a nature walk and looking for nests in nearby trees.

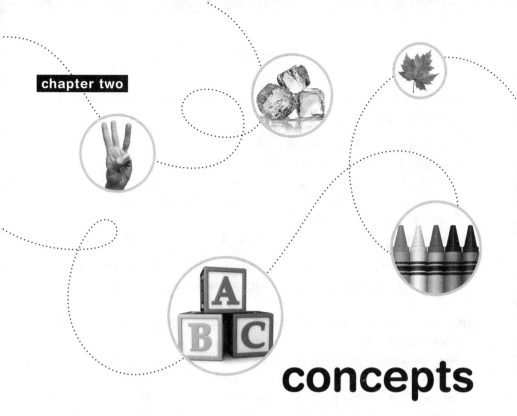

concepts

Ainsworth, Kimberly. *Hootenanny! A Festive Counting Book.*

Illus. Jo Brown. New York: Little Simon, 2011.

Summary: Five owls gather on a Saturday night to party. This counting book focuses only on the numbers 1 through 5.

Action: Dance and party along with the owls. You'll find the lines "Hootenanny, hootenanny—it's time for fun. Hootenanny, hootenanny—the party has begun!" numerous times throughout the text. Be sure to dance and move every time you read those words. If you wish, create a tune to sing them.

Action: Add a counting element to the previous suggested action. When only one owl is at the party, hold up one finger while you dance around. When a second owl joins the party, hold up two fingers while you dance around. By the end of the book, you'll have five fingers up in the air.

Alda, Arlene. *Hello, Good-bye.*

Plattsburgh, NY: Tundra Books, 2009.

Summary: Photographs and one-word descriptors are used to explain a variety of opposites.

Action: Encourage everyone to act out as many of the concepts as possible. For example:

- Shiver for cold and fan yourself for hot.
- Stand up tall for straight and lean to the side for slanted.
- Hold your finger to your lips for quiet and make lots of noise for loud.
- Close your eyes for asleep and move around for awake.
- Pretend to push and pull.
- Stand apart for alone and stand in a group for together.

Note: Some of the pages may not lend themselves to being acted out. It's okay to read some of the pages without including movement.

Brocket, Jane. *1 Cookie, 2 Chairs, 3 Pears: Numbers Everywhere.*
Minneapolis: Millbrook, 2014.
Summary: Learn the numbers from 1 to 20. Each number is featured on a page with one or more photographs depicting that number.
Action: While counting out loud, clap or jump the correct number of times together as a group to further reinforce each number after you read about it. Add a musical element by using shakers to count together.

Brocket, Jane. *Ruby, Violet, Lime: Looking for Color.*
Minneapolis: Millbrook, 2012.
Summary: Photographs illustrate how colors are found all around us. The brief text describes the colors using synonyms, including "ruby," "lemon," and "emerald," and also discusses the concept of primary and secondary colors. Red, yellow, blue, green, orange, purple, brown, pink, black, white, silver, and gold are all featured in the text and photographs.
Action: After reading about each color, ask the children to find that color in your storytime space. Ask questions like "Who is wearing red today?"
Action: Before storytime, create paper circles for each of the colors mentioned in the book. Tape these circles to the walls of your storytime space. After reading about each color, ask everyone to get up and move to stand underneath the matching circle. Stand in front of the group to read about the next color and then move to the next color. Continue until the entire book has been read. Put the colors on the wall in the same order as they can be found in the book, or make the activity more difficult by mixing them up.

Action: Give each child a small circle of construction paper for each color mentioned in the book. After you read about each color, ask everyone to hold up the matching piece of construction paper.

Carole, Bonnie. *Black and White in Winter.*
North Mankato, MN: Rourke Educational Media, 2015.

———. *Blue and Yellow in Summer.*
North Mankato, MN: Rourke Educational Media, 2015.

———. *Brown and Orange in Fall.*
North Mankato, MN: Rourke Educational Media, 2015.

———. *Red and Green in Spring.*
North Mankato, MN: Rourke Educational Media, 2015.

Summary: Each title focuses on two colors that are prevalent in a particular season. To further solidify knowledge of the colors, multiple seasonal objects are shown for readers to identify the color.

Action: Give everyone a paper circle for the two colors featured in the book you have chosen to share (for example, a black and a white circle for the winter title). Have kids raise the correct color circle for each color question before you flip the page for the answer.

Action: Choose just one color per book to focus on while reading. Give everyone a movement to do whenever they hear you say that color; tell them not to move when they hear the other color. The photographs in the book act as a preview of what is to come, so this activity focuses on both listening and visual skills.

Dahl, Michael. *Eggs and Legs: Counting by Twos.*
Illus. Todd Ouren. Minneapolis: Picture Window Books, 2005.

———. *Footprints in the Snow: Counting by Twos.*
Illus. Todd Ouren. Minneapolis: Picture Window Books, 2005.

Summary: A hen searches through the farmyard for her eggs, which have started to hatch. A cardinal and a chipmunk follow a set of footprints through the snow, counting by twos all the way to 20.

Action: Stand up and stomp the number of footprints on each page. Be sure to count out loud to further aid in learning numbers. You can also clap or use instruments to count through the book.

Delessert, Etienne. *Full Color.*

Mankato, MN: Creative Editions, 2008.

> **Summary:** Each of the colors of the rainbow has a personality, and then they mix together and create something new. This is a whimsical look at the colors of the world.
>
> **Action:** Give everyone a paper circle for all the colors of the rainbow. Ask them to hold up the correct circle when it is mentioned in the book.
>
> **Action:** Give everyone a piece of translucent red, yellow, and blue tissue paper. When the colors start mixing together, have them hold the correct two colors together to make green, purple, and orange. They may have to hold the tissue paper up to a light to see the color change clearly. What happens when they put all three pieces of paper together?
>
> **Action:** Model ways that everyone can act like each of the colors in the book:
>
> - Hunch your shoulders and look shy like blushing red.
> - Flutter your fingers rapidly like a raging orange fire.
> - Make a big circle above your head with your arms like a yellow sun.
> - Stand your fingers straight up from the ground like a field of green grass.
> - Slap your hands on the ground like you are splashing in blue water.
> - Pull your freshly dyed indigo shirt out of a tub. Be careful not to splash dye on your clothes.
> - Pretend to smell a sweet violet tulip.

Fielding, Beth. *Animal Colors: A Rainbow of Colors from Animals around the World.*

Waynesville, NC: EarlyLight Books, 2009.

> **Summary:** From red to purple, to yellow and orange, to rainbow, each page features photographs of animals in each basic color or color combination.
>
> **Action:** Help everyone identify colors while you read aloud just the names of the animals on each page. When you get to the "red" page, ask everyone that is wearing red to stand up. Then ask everyone to sit down again. Do the same thing with the "orange" page, and so on.
>
> **Action:** Many packs of juggling scarves come in many different colors. Give everyone a juggling scarf and have participants sit so the colors are spread throughout the room. When the color that matches a participant's scarf shows up in the book, have them raise their scarf up high.

Action: Give everyone an instrument to play. Ask them to play their instrument when you get to the page with their favorite color. Remember that many people have multiple favorite colors or may just like playing their instrument for each page. That is okay—they are still interacting with the book.

Jocelyn, Marthe. *Same Same.*

Illus. Tom Slaughter. Plattsburgh, NY: Tundra Books, 2009.

Summary: Look at sets through a very simple lens. Kids are learning to group objects, and this puts the concept on their level.

Action: Show everyone how they can pretend they are part of each set:

- Round: Make a circle with your fingers or make your whole body round.
- Make music: Sing or make noise.
- Fly: Flap your arms like you are flying or hold your arms out straight and soar like an airplane.
- Striped: Use your hands to draw pretend stripes on your body.
- Long: Make your body as long and tall as possible.
- Go: Move around the room.
- Water: Pretend to swim.
- Big: Make your body as big as possible.
- Four legs: Crawl.
- Red: Find something red in the room.

Action: Pay attention closely: each new set contains something from the previous set. For example, "round things" has an apple, the world, and a tambourine. The next set is "things that make music," and it contains a tambourine, a guitar, and a bird. Can you (or the participants) identify the repeat on every page? Pretend to play with or be that item:

- Tambourine: Make a tambourine sound while shaking your hand like you are holding a tambourine.
- Bird: Flap your wings and tweet.
- Bee: Pretend your finger is a bee and buzz it in the air.
- Snake: Hold your arms tight by your side and wiggle like a snake.
- Train: Make a choo-choo sound.
- Boat: Pretend your hand is a boat and move it up and down like it is going over waves.

- Whale: Pretend to dive deep and then come up for air.
- Elephant: Hold your arm up to your nose like you have a long trunk.
- Chair: Sit down.
- Apple (this is the hard one because it cycles back to the first set): Pretend to eat an apple.

Jones, Christianne C. *Splish, Splash, and Blue.*

Illus. Todd Ouren. Minneapolis: Picture Window Books, 2007.

Summary: Take a trip to a water park to find a world filled with blue—blue water, blue towels, blue sky, and more.

Action: Give everyone a piece of paper and a blue crayon. Ask them to draw something that is blue while you read the book.

Action: Give everyone a piece of blue fabric (the pieces can be all different shades of blue if you wish). There are many times in the text when they can use the fabric to mimic the story:

- Hold the fabric high over your head to make a blue sky.
- Flip the fabric back and forth to make a zigzag slide.
- Hold the fabric close as if it is a mat for riding down a slide.
- Make large movements with your arms while holding the fabric to create waves.
- Hold the fabric close over your head as a sun umbrella.
- Use the fabric like a towel.

Jordan, Apple. *Empty Full.*

New York: Marshall Cavendish Benchmark, 2012.

Summary: The concepts of empty and full are easy to understand when you see photographs of a bowl, wagon, bottle, cart, and basket each empty and full. The trim size of this book is small, and it will probably work best with a smaller group.

Action: Give everyone a plastic cup and a small pom-pom. Act out the book together by putting the pom-pom in the cup on the full pages and taking it out for empty pages. A clear plastic cup can help further the understanding of these opposite concepts.

Action: Before storytime, create twelve-inch-diameter circles on the floor using masking tape. Make sure to spread the circles out so that kids can jump out of their circle without jumping into another circle. Have everyone act out the book using their whole body, jumping into the circle for the "full" pages and out of the circle for the "empty" pages.

Jordan, Apple. *Hot Cold.*
New York: Marshall Cavendish Benchmark, 2012.

Summary: Is an oven hot or cold? What about a refrigerator? What about some favorite foods like soup or ice cream? It's easy to tell with simple text and photographs. The trim size of this book is small, and it will probably work best with a smaller group.

Action: Make a fan for everyone by folding a piece of paper accordion style, then pinching it at one end (if time allows, you can let everyone make and decorate their own fan). Whenever something hot is shown in the book, everyone can fan themselves to cool off. If you wish, add a shivering motion to the pages featuring cold.

Action: Give everyone an article of clothing that they can easily put on and take off, such as a hat or a scarf. You can also use a jugging scarf or piece of fabric to act as a blanket. Take the clothing or blanket off on "hot" pages and put it back on for "cold" pages.

Action: Use ice cubes to create a quick, fun extension of this book on a warm, sunny day. Go outside and put your hand on a sidewalk. Is it hot? Now feel the ice cube. Is it cold? Put the ice cube on the sidewalk and watch it melt.

Jordan, Apple. *Noisy Quiet.*
New York: Marshall Cavendish Benchmark, 2012.

Summary: The opposite concepts of noisy and quiet are simply defined in contrasting photographs. An intimate storytime space may be better for the small trim size of this title.

Action: The simplest way to add movement is to allow everyone to be noisy for three seconds to correspond with every noisy page. Before you start reading the book, you may want to practice doing a 3–2–1 countdown to silence for the quiet pages.

Action: Use instruments (maracas, rhythm sticks, bells, etc.) as noisemakers on all the noisy pages.

Action: Make noises that complement the noises illustrated in the book's photographs:

- Pretend to use a party noisemaker. What does it sound like?
- Bang on the floor to mimic a hammer.
- Rev your engines for the four-wheeler.
- Make a noise like a baby crying.
- Lastly, make your favorite noise.

Kaiser, Ruth. *The Smiley Book of Colors.*

New York: Golden Books, 2012.

Summary: Smiley faces are all around. You can find them inside strawberries and apples, on hats, or up in a cloudy sky. An inspirational message accompanies photographs depicting smiles on found objects. You can also explore colors, as each page features a new one.

Action: How many different ways can you smile? Try making a different smiley face at the end of each page. Try these different methods: with your teeth showing, without your teeth showing, using just your eyes, a laughing smile, a confused smile, making a smile using your hands, and making your whole body smile.

Action: Create your own version of this book while it is being read aloud. Give everyone a piece of paper and a crayon. Ask everyone to draw a smile while you read. At the end of the book, group all the pictures by color.

Action: The real stars of this book are the photographs. Focus on them by slowly turning the pages while playing the song "Happy" by Pharrell Williams. Encourage everyone to dance along with the song.

Kalman, Bobbie. *When I Am Happy.*

New York: Crabtree Publishing, 2011.

Summary: What makes you happy? And how do you act? Photographs of real kids demonstrate this positive attitude.

Action: Play or pretend along with the kids in the book. Smile, laugh, clap, dance, hug, kiss, act funny, jump and shout, read, and bake as you read the corresponding pages.

Action: The last double-page spread asks, "What do you say when you are happy?" Sing "If You're Happy and You Know It" and ask for suggestions for verses.

Mamada, Mineko. *Which Is Round? Which Is Bigger?*

Tonawanda, NY: Kids Can Press, 2013.

Summary: A unique way of showing kids that things are not always what they seem. A duck may appear larger than a peacock—until that peacock spreads his feathers. Now who is bigger? This small book is filled with surprising shapes, sizes, and speeds.

Action: Show how each item can fulfill the quality in the question:

- Apple: Make a circle with your hands.
- Pangolin: Roll your body up in a ball.
- Duck: Make yourself big.
- Peacock: Make yourself bigger than the duck by spreading your arms (feathers) out wide.
- Snake: Stand tall and long.
- Ants: Use one finger to point to many spots along a line as if there are many, many ants in a line that is longer than the snake.
- Dog: Run quickly in place.
- Snail: Imitate the quickly rolling snail by rolling your arms like you are doing "The Wheels on the Bus."
- Cat: Climb high up a tree.
- Squirrel: Time to climb higher.
- Apple: Once again, make a circle with your hands.
- Watermelon: Crack open that circle to show what is inside.

Markle, Sandra. *How Many Baby Pandas?*

New York: Walker, 2009.

Summary: Counting is fun when you are counting baby pandas in a photograph. Unlike many counting books, this one stops at the number 8. Each page also features additional information about pandas that families can share when reading the book one-on-one with their children.

Action: Count the baby pandas together on every page. Clap or shake a maraca for every number. Shake the maraca once when you count to 1. Shake it twice when you count to 2.

Action: Helps kids start to recognize the numbers 1 through 8 as they are written. Give everyone a die-cut for each number. You can also use magnetic numbers or large numbers written clearly on index cards. On the page with one panda, show everyone what a number 1 looks like and ask everyone to hold up that number. This activity may take some coaching, so enlist the help of parents and caregivers if possible.

Meredith, Susan Markowitz. *Left or Right?*
Vero Beach, FL: Rourke, 2011.

Summary: Using photographs, this title teaches and tests a child's knowledge of left and right.

Action: There are five times when the book tests the reader's knowledge of left and right. On each of those pages, have everyone raise the hand that they believe gives the right answer. Ask them to keep those hands in the air until the page is turned and the correct answer is revealed. (Note: if you choose to model this activity, remember to raise the opposite hand because children will mirror your actions.)

Miller, Connie Colwell. *Happy Is . . .*
North Mankato, MN: Capstone, 2012.

Summary: Rhyming text describes all the things that can make us happy. Double-page photographs show kids in lots of happy places.

Action: Give everyone a paper plate and a crayon. Ask them to draw a happy face while you read the book.

Action: Pages 18–19 talk about grooving to a happy beat. Play "Happy" by Pharrell Williams or "Don't Worry, Be Happy" by Bobby McFerrin and dance to the beat. You can play just part of the song or the whole thing. Depending on the age of your group, you may wish to guide the dance party: "Let's wave our happy arms in the air," "Let's stomp our happy feet," or "Let's twist."

Nunn, Daniel. *Animals Big and Small.*
Chicago: Raintree, 2012.

Summary: Photographs of real animals are set against a cartoon-like background to explain the concepts of big/small, tall/short, long/short, and wide/narrow.

Action: Act out each of the descriptors used in the book. Ask everyone to make themselves big, small, tall, short, long, wide, and narrow to match the animals.

Oldland, Nicholas. *Dinosaur Countdown.*

Tonawanda, NY: Kids Can Press, 2012.

Summary: Count down from 10 to 0 with velociraptors, Deinosuchus, and Parasaurolophus (a pronunciation guide is included in the back of the book). The illustrations are placed against a crisp white background, making them easier to count.

Action: Place felt numbers from 10 to 0 on your flannelboard. Count down along with the book. When you get to "nine lazing deinosuchus," ask a storytime participant to come up and remove the 10 from your flannelboard. Continue until only the 0 is left.

Action: Give everyone ten identical items (ten die-cut dinosaur shapes, ten cotton balls, ten paper circles, etc.). Place ten items on your flannelboard so that the group can see and copy you. Line up the ten items in front of each person. Read "ten striding velociraptors," then count the ten items together taking care to point to each one. Read the next page and say, "There are only nine now—put one of your dinosaurs/cotton balls/paper circles behind your back. Let's count to nine together." Continue until there is nothing left.

Action: Give everyone an instrument to play as they count. After reading each page, count to the correct number, playing the instrument as you count. Kids are accustomed to counting forward, not backward, so don't be surprised if there are a few mistakes as they learn the pattern.

Pallotta, Jerry. *Butterfly Counting.*

Illus. Shennen Bersani. Watertown, MA: Charlesbridge, 2015.

Summary: Colors, numbers, butterfly facts, and the word "butterfly" in different languages—this title packs it all in. Also unique is the fact that this book counts up to 25, continuing on beyond the typical 10.

Action: Give everyone twenty-five die-cut butterflies. Use the die-cuts to count along with the book: pick up one die-cut for the page with one butterfly, two for the page with two butterflies, and so on. Be sure to count out loud on each page to help kids learn their numbers. Don't feel like counting all the way to 25? Stop at whatever number works best for you.

Action: Numbers 1 through 10 also focus on different colors: red, blue, green, purple, orange, black, white, pink, yellow, and brown. Say to the group, "Are you wearing red? Stand up if you are wearing the color that matches the butterfly on this page." Prompt the group in the same way with each color.

PatrickGeorge, *I Hear . . .*
Kent, United Kingdom: PatrickGeorge, 2012.

Summary: What do your ears do? See a variety of things that your ears can hear throughout the day.

Action: Make noises and act out every page in this book:

- Bee: Make a buzzing sound while pretending that your pointer finger is a bee.
- Bird: Flap your wings and tweet like a bird.
- Slurping: Make a slurping sound while pretending to drink from a glass.
- Thunder: Stomp your feet while making a loud, thundering boom.
- Low notes: Crouch down low while making a low-pitched sound.
- High notes: Stand on your tiptoes while making a high-pitched sound.
- Branch: Use your hand to pretend to break a branch in half while making a cracking sound.
- Heart: Say "thump-thump" while gently patting your hand over your heart.
- Child: Cry like a baby.
- Balloon: Create an open circle using your hands, then make a large "pop" sound while quickly moving your hands apart.
- Drums: Pretend to hold drum sticks and bang on a large drum while making a booming sound.
- Footsteps: Make a crunching sound each time you take a step.
- Plane: Pretend your hand is a plane flying through the air while you make a plane sound.
- Crowd: Hold your hands above your head in triumph while cheering.
- Phone: Hold a pretend phone up to your ear while it rings.
- Waves: Make crashing waves with your hands while making a whooshing sound.
- Train: Pull down on a pretend train horn while saying, "Choo, choo."
- Alarm: Shake your whole body while making a loud beeping sound.

- Nothing: Hold your finger up to your mouth and don't make a sound.
- Laughter: Hold your belly while you laugh loudly.

PatrickGeorge. *I Smell . . .*
Kent, United Kingdom: PatrickGeorge, 2012.

Summary: Part of a series of books about the five senses, this book makes you think about all the things you smell throughout the day. Are they good smells? Or bad smells?

Action: Pause after reading each page to talk about whether it is a good smell or a bad smell. Ask participants, "What does the scent make you want to do?" For example, cupcakes baking may make you rub your tummy with delight, whereas dinner burning might make you flap your hand in front of your nose to waft the smell away. Make a face or do a movement for each scent. Some scents, such as fish, may invoke varying reactions from different storytime participants.

Action: Bring along some of the items in the book so that participants can smell them as you get to that page. (This will probably work best with a smaller group.) Scents featured in the book that are easy to bring to storytime are: lemons, clean socks, freshly cut grass (just pull a few pieces of grass from your yard), a flower, cheese (the stinkier the better for this activity), bubble bath (pour some bubble bath liquid in a small cup), and an onion (cut it to make it more pungent).

PatrickGeorge. *I Taste . . .*
Kent, United Kingdom: PatrickGeorge, 2012.

Summary: Your mouth can taste all sorts of things, from sour to sweet to spicy. Explore how different things taste through cartoon illustrations. Consider your audience before reading this book—there is one page that shows a cartoon vampire and bat and the words "your blood!" It won't bother most kids, but it may ruffle feathers for some adults.

Action: Create two movements, one for things you like to eat and one for things you don't like to eat. For example, throw your arms up in the air and shout "Hooray" for things you do like to eat. Cover your mouth to protect yourself from things you don't like to eat. Ask everyone to show their feelings for each of the items in this book. How many people like sour lemons? What about broccoli? Surely everyone likes ice cream.

Action: Sing a modified version of "If You're Happy and You Know It" for every page of the book:

> If you're hungry and you know it, eat a lollipop (yum, yum).
> If you're hungry and you know it, eat a lollipop (yum, yum).
> If you're hungry and you know it,
> A lollipop ought to solve it.
> If you're hungry and you know it, eat a lollipop (yum, yum).

Create your own movements for each page. Examples may include puckering your face for a lemon, slurping for spaghetti, or saying "eww" for a worm.

Rotner, Shelley. *Senses in the City.*
Minneapolis: Millbrook, 2008.

———. *Senses on the Farm.*
Minneapolis: Millbrook, 2009.
> **Summary:** There are lots of ways you can use your five senses in a city or on a farm. Take a photographic trip to explore city or farm life.
> **Action:** Learn more about the five senses by pointing to the correct body part each time one of the senses is mentioned in book:
>
> - See: Point to your eyes.
> - Touch: Point to your hand.
> - Hear: Point to your ears.
> - Smell: Point to your nose.
> - Taste: Point to your mouth.

Stewart, Melissa. *Why Are Animals Blue?*
Berkeley Heights, NJ: Enslow Elementary, 2009.

———. *Why Are Animals Green?*
Berkeley Heights, NJ: Enslow Elementary, 2009.

———. *Why Are Animals Orange?*
Berkeley Heights, NJ: Enslow Elementary, 2009.

————. *Why Are Animals Purple?*
Berkeley Heights, NJ: Enslow Elementary, 2009.

————. *Why Are Animals Red?*
Berkeley Heights, NJ: Enslow Elementary, 2009.

————. *Why Are Animals Yellow?*
Berkeley Heights, NJ: Enslow Elementary, 2009.

Summary: Each title features animals with the title color. Readers will learn about common and uncommon animals in all of their favorite colors.

Action: Give each child a blank piece of paper and a crayon that matches the title you are reading. While you read the book, ask them to draw a picture of their favorite animal that matches the color crayon.

Action: Read through the entire book, sharing all the colorful animals. After reading, say that you are going to look through the book a second time. This time, ask kids to raise their hands when you get to the page with their favorite animal in the book. This is a great way to delve deeper into the book on a preschool-appropriate level.

Stills, Caroline. *Mice Mischief: Math Facts in Action.*
Illus. Judith Rossell. New York: Holiday House, 2013.

Summary: How many different ways can you add two numbers to get 10? Follow along as ten comical mice slowly go from doing their chores to playing.

Action: Each time a number is mentioned, hold up that many fingers. So, on the first page, you will hold up all ten fingers. On the second double-page spread, hold up nine fingers as the mice tidy their beds. Then hold up one finger as a single mouse somersaults. Continue this way throughout the book as a way to lay basic groundwork for the understanding of addition.

Action: Let the math become secondary as you play with the mice. Give everyone a juggling scarf to interact with on each page:

- Use the scarf like a blanket and then stretch as you wake up.
- Use the scarf like a blanket again and pretend to make your bed.
- Throw the scarf up in the air like you are flipping a pancake.
- Use the scarf like a sponge and pretend to wash dishes.

- Hold tight to two corners of the scarf as if you have hung it out on a line to dry.
- Fold the scarf like laundry.
- Use the scarf to scrub the floor.
- Hold one tip of the scarf and sweep the other on the floor like a mop.
- Hold one tip of the scarf and wave the other in the air as if you are dusting something.
- Rub the scarf on your arm like you are polishing silver.
- Throw all the scarves up in the air at the same time to play.

Zuckerman, Andrew. *Creature ABC.*

San Francisco: Chronicle Books, 2009.

> **Summary:** An alphabet book with stunning photographs of animals against a crisp white background. Many of the letter pages show only a portion of the animal, which creates a guessing game until you turn the page. A few letters stand for something other than a specific animal; for example, "Nn" is for "nocturnal."

> **Action:** So many pages offer an opportunity to guess the animal before you turn the page. Pause before revealing the animal to let the kids act like their guess. For example, "Aa" is for "alligator." Kids can open their arms up wide and chomp down like an alligator. Or they may choose to crawl/slither around on the floor.

> **Action:** Use this book over multiple weeks by featuring one letter a week. For the first week, show the "Aa" pages and give the kids a die-cut "A" or a sheet of paper with a clear "A" on it. (While slightly more advanced, you may give attendees examples of both upper and lower case letters if you wish.) They can trace the letter with their fingers. Continue the following week with "Bb," and so on.

construction and things that go

Amstutz, Lisa J. *Bike Safety: A Crash Course.*
North Mankato, MN: Capstone, 2014.

Summary: It can be fun to ride a bike, but you need to make sure to follow simple safety rules. This is a brief introduction to riding a bike safely. With balance bikes becoming more popular, kids can ride bikes even younger than before so this is important information for them to learn early.

Action: Go along for the ride, but be sure to be careful along the way:

- Put on your helmet.
- Tie your shoelaces.
- Feel the tires. Do they feel firm? If not, pump them up.
- Get on your bike. Can you touch the pedals and the handlebars?
- Time to cross the street. Hop off your bike and walk it across.
- Watch where you are going.
- Practice hand signals for a left turn, right turn, and stop.

Aylmore, Angela. *We Work at the Fire Station.*

Chicago: Heinemann Library, 2006.

Summary: Spend a day at the firehouse and learn how firefighters put out fires and rescue people.

Action: Before storytime, create a fake fire by piling up pieces of red, orange, and yellow paper. Cover up the fire with fabric or a box. When the "alarm rings" in the book, uncover the fake fire so everyone can see it. Flip to the next page and have everyone pretend to put on their safety gear. When you get to pages 14–15, give everyone a piece of blue paper signifying water. Have everyone come up and throw their water on the fire to put it out. Once the fire is covered in blue paper, finish the book. Definitely focus on page 21 and stress that kids should never go near a real fire.

Bridges, Sarah. *I Drive a Bulldozer.*

Illus. Derrick Alderman and Denise Shea. Minneapolis: Picture Window Books, 2005.

Summary: Cartoon illustrations and simple text introduce kids to these strong construction machines. Captions provide more information on each page that you may wish to share with eager learners.

Action: Act out the book as you read:

- Pretend to put on your safety equipment.
- Check the gears then pull yourself into the seat.
- Turn the key to get it started.
- Making a beeping noise while backing up.
- Pretend to scrape the ground. Get down on your knees and put your hands in front of you like they are a plow. Lower them to the ground and pretend to push dirt out of the way.
- Then push a big tree out of the way. *Timber!*
- Shake your whole body as you wiggle in your seat.
- Take a break to eat a pretend sandwich. Don't let it get too hot on the hood.
- Clean off the tracks and head home for the day.

Bridges, Sarah. *I Drive a Crane.*

Illus. Amy Bailey Muehlenhardt. Minneapolis: Picture Window Books, 2006.

Summary: Cranes can be taller than fifteen-story buildings, and they need someone special to run them each day. Spend a day with a crane operator.

Action: Join the crane operator in his work:

- Climb up the ladder to the cab. Don't just climb for three seconds; keep going for a little while because it is a long way up.
- Get settled into your seat.
- Sway from side to side as the wind moves the crane a little.
- Lower the cable to the ground. Do this by pretending to maneuver a lever. This is a great opportunity for sound effects.
- Lift the heavy object with the crane. For this part, pretend you are the crane rather than the operator. Hold your arm out and pretend to lift something very heavy.
- Climb back down to the ground. Remember, this takes a while.

Bridges, Sarah. *I Drive a Freight Train.*

Illus. Amy Bailey Muehlenhardt. Minneapolis: Picture Window Books, 2006.

Summary: Ride along with an engineer and conductor as they describe how a train drives across the country. Each page has a simple storyline to follow and a caption with further information. Read one or both sections based on the interest and age level of your group.

Action: Everyone likes acting like a train. Bend your arms at your elbows and move your arms in circles like the wheels on a train. Do this while making a train "whoo-whoo" sound at the end of each page.

Action: Hook two paper plates together with a dowel (or a drinking straw) and tape so that they look like train wheels. Give every child two sets of plates (one for each side of the train) and let them pretend to be a train while you read the book. Hint: You may want to use dessert-size paper plates so that the dowels are long enough to reach the center of each plate.

Bridges, Sarah. *I Drive a Garbage Truck.*

Illus. Derrick Alderman and Denise Shea. Minneapolis: Picture Window Books, 2005.

Summary: Spend a day with a garbage truck to learn what the workers do. More information is provided as captions on the cartoon illustrations.

Action: Give everyone a copy of a photograph of a garbage bag. You may instead choose to give everyone construction paper cut to look like a sealed garbage bag. On pages 10–11, the book tells readers that the garbage is emptied into the back of the truck. Pause reading to walk through the area with a wagon or cart that can serve as a garbage truck. Ask everyone to toss their bag into the truck.

Carr, Aaron. *Jumbo Jets.*
New York: AV2 by Weigl, 2014.

Summary: Fly high in the skies with these huge planes. Quick, bite-sized facts are included on every page. More information for each double-page spread is provided in the back.

Action: Pretend to fly with the planes in the book. Tell everyone to pay close attention to the photographs—is the plane in the air or on the ground? The book starts with a photograph of a plane in the air. Hold out your arms as wings, take a couple steps forward, and lift off. On the very next page, the airplane in the photograph is on the ground. Start your descent by leaning forward and bending closer to the ground. Stay on the ground until the next time you see a photograph with a plane in flight (pages 12–13) and pretend to lift off again.

Action: After reading pages 18–19, pause to play "Hail to the Chief" and have everyone pretend to walk down the steps from Air Force One as if they are the president. Don't forget to wave to the news reporters.

Carr, Aaron. *Monster Trucks.*
New York: AV2 by Weigl, 2014.

Summary: Large photographs and spare text provide information about this high-interest topic.

Action: Every time you read the word "monster," have everyone make a scary face like a monster. This activity will help to increase listening skills as they pay attention waiting for the next time "monster" is said.

Action: Focus on the huge size of monster trucks for another listening activity. Every time you read the words "monster trucks," have everyone try to make their body as large as possible.

Feldman, Thea. *Trains.*

New York: Kingfisher, 2012.

Summary: A beginning-to-read title filled with information and photographs of many types of trains.

Action: The trains in this book travel in many different places. Pretend you are the train on these pages:

- Pages 6–7: Travel across the desert. Trains don't have eyes, but cover yours so you don't get sand in them.
- Pages 8–9: Create a tunnel over your head using your arms as you go through the tunnel.
- Pages 10–11: Look over the sides. Ask the children, "Can you see anything in the water under the bridge?"
- Pages 12–13: Go through another tunnel.
- Pages 14–15: Pretend to dip down underground.
- Pages 16–17: Slow to a stop.
- You can continue reading the rest of the book, or leave the remainder for a family that is interested in the book.

Lindeen, Mary. *Helicopters.*

Minneapolis: Bellwether Media, 2008.

Summary: Part of the Blastoff! Readers series. Kids can see photographs of helicopters in action and learn about the different types of things they are used for.

Action: Give everyone a juggling scarf so they can become a helicopter. Show them how to hold on to one end and spin it above their heads like a rotor to make their helicopter fly. Tell everyone to make their helicopter fly whenever the photograph shows a helicopter flying. Keep the rotor still when the helicopter in the photograph is sitting on land. Be sure to instruct everyone to be careful of their neighbor as they whip their juggling scarf above their head.

Moss, Jenny. *Look Inside a Castle.*

Mankato, MN: Capstone, 2010.

Summary: How were castles built, and who lived in them? Photographs and art will help kids understand these buildings that fascinate many.

Action: Page 14 talks about parties being held in the great hall. Pause reading to play a couple minutes of music so you can have a quick party in your great storytime hall.

Action: The first page talks about castles keeping kings and nobles safe. Give everyone a shield so they can help protect the castle. A cheap and easy shield can be a paper plate with a piece of paper or ribbon taped to the back as a handle. At the end of each page, ask everyone if the castle is still protected. Encourage them to raise their shields in agreement. If time allows, you may wish to let everyone decorate their shields with crayons or markers.

Murrell, Deborah, and Christiane Gunzi. *Mega Trucks: The Biggest, Toughest Trucks in the World.*

New York: Scholastic, 2005.

Summary: This book is big in size and big in trucks. The pages are full of information but you can read just the largest font to share loggers, diggers, loaders, concrete mixers, and more trucks during a storytime.

Action: Give everyone a paper plate with the center cut out as a pretend steering wheel. Also give them a rhythm stick with which they can pretend is whatever lever their truck needs. At the end of each page, have everyone pretend to drive that truck. For the transporters and loggers, you can drive your steering wheel and shift gears. Use the rhythm stick as a lever to control the bucket on the digger, dump the load out of the giant dump trucks, or turn on the back of the concrete mixer.

Prince, April Jones. *What Do Wheels Do All Day?*

Illus. Giles Laroche. Boston: Houghton Mifflin, 2006.

Summary: Wheels are all over the place—on cars, bicycles, and strollers, even high in the sky as a Ferris wheel. Brief rhyming text describes wheels spinning, zooming, and rolling.

Action: Give everyone a paper plate to use as a steering wheel. Show each page. Does the illustration have a vehicle with a steering wheel? If so, have participants pretend to drive a car (or other vehicle). You may want to prompt kids on each page. (For example: "Does the bus have a steering wheel? Yes, it does. Let's drive the bus. Does the skateboard have a steering wheel? No, we drive it with our feet.") Note that bicycles may be confusing to kids because you steer them, but with handlebars, not with a steering wheel.

Action: The page that reads "Wheels carry travelers," features a picture of a bus. Pause reading to sing a couple verses of "The Wheels on the Bus."

Action: At the end of each page, have everyone roll their arms like you do for "The Wheels on the Bus" to signify wheels rolling.

Riggs, Kate. *Jets.*
Mankato, MN: Creative Education / Creative Paperbacks, 2015.

———. *Motorcycles.*
Mankato, MN: Creative Education / Creative Paperbacks, 2015.

———. *Speedboats.*
Mankato, MN: Creative Education / Creative Paperbacks, 2015.

———. *Stock Cars.*
Mankato, MN: Creative Education / Creative Paperbacks, 2015.

Summary: All four titles use action filled photographs and minimal text to describe these fast and exciting machines.

Action: Put your hands on the handlebars or the steering wheel and rev your engines at the end of each page. For the *Jets* book, put your arms out wide and fly at the end of each page. For the *Speedboats* book, you can pretend your hand is a boat and make it go zooming past you at the end of each page.

Action: For the *Jets* book, use masking tape to mark a runway on the floor. On pages 16–17, the readers see a photo of jets on a runway ready to take off. Let everyone take a turn running down the runway and pretending to lift off. The very next double-page spread reads "Go, jet, go!"—you may wish to read this page as each child takes a turn.

Action: For the *Motorcycles* book, pay attention to the photographs. Do you need to lean into a turn? Which way should you lean to match the photograph?

Action: Don't forget to put on your pretend lifejacket and helmet before starting the *Speedboats* book. Take them back off and hang them up to dry when the book is done.

Action: For the *Stock Cars* book, pay attention to the photographs. Is the car moving or sitting still? Roll your arms (like "The Wheels on the Bus") on every page that the car is moving.

Riggs, Kate. *Time to Build.*

Illus. Laszlo Kubinyi. Mankato, MN: Creative Editions, 2015.

> **Summary:** Watch as a pile of lumber becomes a tree house with the help of a tape measure, saw, wrench, drill, screwdriver, and hammer. This is a board book, but the illustrations are quite large.
>
> **Action:** Pretend to use all the tools along with the people in the book.
>
> **Action:** Focus on one tool and spend a lot of time pretending to use it. For example, you can give everyone a rhythm stick that they can pretend is a hammer. When you get to the page with the hammer, tell everyone that there are lots of nails and we need everyone's help. Hammer the pretend nails into the floor. You can also use a rhythm stick as a pretend screwdriver and twist your wrist to use it.

Schuh, Mari. *Fire Trucks in Action.*

Mankato, MN: Capstone, 2009.

> **Summary:** Learn about different types of fire trucks and the equipment firefighters use.
>
> **Action:** Fire trucks have red flashing lights to help people see them as they rush to a fire. Give every child a piece of red construction paper cut into a circle. Show them how to hold up the circle and wave it to look like a flashing red light. Flash the lights at the end of every page to pretend you are a fire truck.
>
> **Action:** Pretend to put on turn-out gear before you start reading the book; put on your pants, jacket, boots, and fire helmet. Then act out the pages to pretend you are a firefighter. If funds allow, give everyone a plastic fire hat from a party store.
>
> - Drive to the fire.
> - Pull the hose off of the truck.
> - Hop on the back of the fire truck.
> - Hook the hose up to a fire hydrant.
> - Climb the ladder.
> - Grab an axe or saw from the fire truck.
> - Find a Band-Aid and pretend to put it on.
> - Use a big tool to cut into a car.
> - Park the fire truck back at the station.

Troupe, Thomas Kingsley. *Blow It Up!*
North Mankato, MN: Capstone, 2014.

Summary: Kaboom! Crash! Blam! Come along as workers blow up an empty building, an old stadium, and a weak bridge.

Action: Pause reading and sing a modified version of "If You're Happy and You Know It" as each building is blown up. Be sure to make loud, energetic crashing and booming sounds:

> If it's an empty building and you know it, blow it up (boom, crash!).
> If it's an empty building and you know it, blow it up (boom, crash!).
> If it's an empty building no one uses,
> Then it's time to light the fuse.
> If it's an empty building and you know it, blow it up (boom, crash!).
>
> If it's an old stadium and you know it . . .
> If it's a weak bridge and you know it . . .

Action: Comic book–style phrases are used throughout to add excitement to the text. When you read "KaBOOM!," "CRASH!," "BLAM!," and "BA-DOOM! BOOM! BOOM!," have everyone join in. Be sure to crumple to the ground like a building that has been blown up after each one.

Troupe, Thomas Kingsley. *Crush It!*
North Mankato, MN: Capstone, 2014.

Summary: Take a trip to the scrap yard to watch old cars get crushed so the metal can be recycled.

Action: Tell kids that they can be a car crusher too. Ask them to get their hands ready by holding one hand a couple inches above the other. Make sure the palms are facing each other. Crush a pretend car on all of the pages that the crusher is working hard.

Action: Do you have a bunch of matchbox cars? Kids can pretend to crunch one throughout the book. Be careful about using cheap plastic cars that may actually crush and hurt someone.

Action: A simple die-cut paper car can add fun to this book. Give one to every participant to crush flat between their hands. Each time the crusher in the book goes to work, crush the car so that paper crinkles and folds. By the end of the book they'll have a flat, crumpled piece of paper.

Troupe, Thomas Kingsley. *Knock It Down!*

North Mankato, MN: Capstone, 2014.

Summary: Follow along as a wrecking ball and excavator tear down an old courthouse. The addition of comic book–style "Smash!," "Blam!," and "Whoosh!" makes this a fun read.

Action: Give everyone a pretend wrecking ball before you start the book. A simple wrecking ball can be a large pom-pom with a long string tied to it. Show everyone how to hold up the pom-pom like a wrecking ball, then release it to smash into a pretend building. Now everyone can help tear down the old courthouse.

Action: Give everyone something they can knock down multiple times throughout the book. Ideas include a long, tall block or a plastic cup. Have everyone sit on the floor and put their "building" in front of them. Whenever the wrecking ball smashes into the building, ask them to knock into their "building" with their hand. Did the building get knocked down? If so, they can pick it back up for the next wrecking-ball page.

Troupe, Thomas Kingsley. *Shred It!*

North Mankato, MN: Capstone, 2014.

Summary: Ever wonder how they make rubber playground material? Comic book–style words add a fun element to this book about tearing up tires and bottles to recycle them for other projects.

Action: Give everyone a piece of paper in the shape of a tire (a die-cut "O" will work just fine). When the tires in the book are shredded to pieces, tear up your tires along with the action. At the end of storytime, ask everyone to help you collect the little pieces of paper. Save them in a box to use another time for a snow storytime.

Action: Don't want the mess of lots of little pieces of paper? Everyone can act out the fun words in the book:

- Thunk: Pretend to drop a heavy tire in the shredder.
- Rip and tear: Pretend to tear something to pieces.
- Slash and squeak: Keep tearing things up.

Tuchman, Gail. *Race Day.*

Washington, DC: National Geographic, 2010.

Summary: This "pre-reader" beginning-to-read book features photographs that make you feel like you are a driver in a NASCAR race.

Action: Before reading the book, use tape to create a finish line in your storytime space. Create a green flag and a checkered flag out of paper (you may also be able to find toy ones at a party supply store). Ask everyone to pretend to climb into their cars and put their hands on the wheel. Tell them to wait until they see the green flag. When you get to page 8, wave your green flag and let everyone pretend to drive around the track. They can do this sitting in their seats, or you can let them move around the storytime space. When you get to page 22, wave your checkered flag and ask everyone to cross over the finish line in their cars.

Action: The words "vroom" and "zoom" appear multiple times in the book. Encourage good listening skills by asking everyone to move their hand quickly in front of their body like a car racing past on a race track every time they hear either of those words. You can also make the activity more difficult by creating two different movements for "vroom" and "zoom." For example, they can hold on to their pretend steering wheel and make a sharp turn for "vroom," and move their hand quickly in front of their body for "zoom."

Action: Give everyone a toy car to play with while you read the book. They can drive the cars on the floor in their own mini-race.

Williams, Linda D. *Backhoes.*

North Mankato, MN: Capstone, 2005.

Summary: Kids are always fascinated by construction vehicles, and this book has lots of big pictures to fuel their interest.

Action: Ask everyone to use their hands and arm as the bucket and boom of a backhoe. Pretend to dig whenever the backhoe in the photograph is digging.

Action: Give everyone a handful (or just a couple pieces) of brown confetti to serve as dirt. They can put in on the ground in front of them and pretend to dig in it while you read. When you get to the page when the backhoe dumps dirt into the back of a truck, walk around with a wagon so kids can dump their dirt into the truck. You can also use a box or bag to simulate the truck.

Action: If you are able to read this book outside, give everyone a small cup of clean soil to dig in while you read.

Williams, Linda D. *Bulldozers.*
Mankato, MN: Capstone, 2005.

Summary: Learn about the parts of a bulldozer, then watch them work.

Action: Put a bunch of building blocks around your storytime space. When you get to the page where you learn that bulldozers can push rocks and trees out of the way, ask everyone to help push the "rocks" to the wall or edge of the space. Get on your hands and lower your blades (hands) to the ground. Then slowly push the "rocks" out of the way. Once all of the rocks are safely moved, continue with the remainder of the book.

Action: You may choose to do the previous activity with paper and real rocks. If you choose to use real rocks, look for ones that don't have any pointy or sharp edges. Fold pieces of regular paper in half lengthwise. Hold the paper in your hand like a bulldozer blade. Use the blade to push the rocks out of the way.

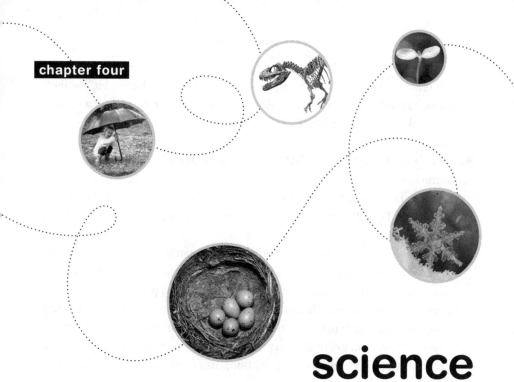

science

Aston, Dianna Hutts. *An Egg Is Quiet.*

Illus. Sylvia Long. San Francisco: Chronicle Books, 2006.

> **Summary:** Large text on each page describes the variety of shapes and sizes of eggs found in nature. Each different egg is labeled on the page for those who want identifying information.
>
> **Action:** Give everyone a copy of the egg outline found in the appendix. Provide crayons so that children can color their own personal egg while you read the story. If you wish, everyone can tear their egg in two on the last page to simulate a hatching egg.

Aston, Dianna Hutts. *A Seed Is Sleepy.*

Illus. Sylvia Long. San Francisco: Chronicle Books, 2007.

> **Summary:** Large text on each page allows the book to be read like a story: a seed is sleepy, fruitful, adventurous, and more. Further information in a smaller font can be shared one-on-one with children who enjoy the book and ask for more. A large variety of seeds and plants are illustrated in ink and watercolor.
>
> **Action:** Have everyone start out curled up close to the floor like an unopened seed. Slowly get bigger and bigger as you read each page until everyone

is reaching high up into the air like sunflowers when the seed is "awake!"

Action: Extend this book after reading it by letting everyone plant a seed in a small cup to bring home.

Barner, Bob. *Dinosaurs ROAR, Butterflies SOAR!*
San Francisco: Chronicle Books, 2009.

Summary: Did you know that butterflies outlasted the dinosaurs? Colorful paper collage illustrations complement the straightforward history of these insects.

Action: Take a few seconds at the end of each page to let everyone pretend they are a butterfly. Flitter around the room throughout the book. Pretend to fly past dinosaurs, woolly mammoths, and people.

Action: Give everyone a die-cut dinosaur and a die-cut butterfly. They can pretend that the butterfly is flying around the dinosaur throughout the book. When you get to the part when the dinosaurs become extinct, put the dinosaur die-cut down on the floor and continue to let the butterfly flitter around.

Cassino, Mark, and Jon Nelson, PhD. *The Story of Snow.*
San Francisco: Chronicle Books, 2009.

Summary: See snow in a new way through photographs of delicate snow crystals. The book includes a large amount of text, but it can be shared with a preschool group by reading just the largest font on each page.

Action: Give everyone a cotton ball to play with as you read the book. Throw the cotton balls up in the air together to make it snow in storytime.

Action: Give everyone a pair of gloves or mittens to wear during the book. (You can most likely get a bunch of cheap gloves or mittens at a dollar store.) Before reading, put on the mittens, then pretend to put on a hat, coat, and snow boots. Take breaks every couple of pages to have everyone pretend to play in the snow: make a snowball, make a snowman, and make a snow angel.

DePalma, Mary Newell. *A Grand Old Tree.*
New York: Arthur A. Levine Books, 2005.

Summary: Follow the life cycle of a tree as it grows, houses animals, bears fruit, and eventually falls to the ground and continues to be a part of nature.

Action: Ask everyone to stand and put their hands up in the air (like the branches of a tree) throughout the book. They can sway in the breeze along with the tree and fall to the ground with the tree.

Action: Give everyone a handful of small pom-poms before you start reading the book. Ask them to tightly hold on to the pom-poms until the right moment. On the page where the tree sows seeds, have everyone throw their pom-poms up in the air so they can see how far a tree's acorns or seeds can spread.

Gerber, Carole. *Spring Blossoms.*

Illus. Leslie Evans. Watertown, MA: Charlesbridge, 2013.

Summary: We often think of flowers growing up from the soil in the garden. This title examines flowers that grow on trees in the spring.

Action: Give everyone a copy of the tree outline from the appendix and some crayons. While you read the story, ask kids to add flowers to the trees.

Action: Toward the back of the book, a rainstorm causes blossoms to fall from the trees. Throw up confetti so everyone can play in a shower of petals. You can also give each child a die-cut flower to throw up in the air at this point in the book.

Goodman, Emily. *Plant Secrets.*

Illus. Phyllis Limbacher Tildes. Watertown, MA: Charlesbridge, 2009.

Summary: From seed to plant to flower to fruit and back to seeds, this book shows the cycle of plants in very simple terms. There is more information in the back for families that wish to share more with their children.

Action: Act out the different stages as a group:

- Seed: Pretend to plant a seed in the ground.
- Plant: Crouch down low and slowly stand up as your plant grows.
- Flower: Hold your hands tight together in two fists. Slowly open up your fingers like a flower blooming.
- Fruit: Pretend to eat some yummy fruit.
- Seed: Plant another seed.

Action: Bring in a seed, plant, flower, and piece of fruit. After you read, "But all these seeds have a SECRET," let everyone touch the seed. Ask them if they know the seed's secret. After a few guesses, continue reading. After you read, "But all of these plants have a SECRET," let everyone touch the plant. Ask them if they know the plant's secret. Continue with the flower and piece of fruit. If you bring a piece of fruit like an apple, cut it open to reveal the secret seeds inside.

Hall, Katharine. *Trees: A Compare and Contrast Book.*
Mt. Pleasant, SC: Arbordale, 2015.

Summary: Large photographs and simple text describe how trees grow in different areas, have varying root bases, and broad or thin leaves.

Action: Use a resource or website such as Signing Savvy (www.signingsavvy .com) to learn the sign for "tree," "tree trunk," "root," and "leaf." When each one is explored in the book, practice the signs together.

Action: There are many pages where the group can pretend to be the trees in the book. Use the following movement suggestions to play along:

- Bunch close together for the many oak trees that live together.
- Spread apart for the acacia tree that lives alone.
- Stand tall while fanning yourself for the trees that live in warm climates.
- Stand tall while shivering for the trees that live in cold climates.
- Squat down to pretend you are a bonsai tree.
- Stand as tall as you can to pretend you are a redwood tree.

Harris, Calvin. *Scarecrows.*
Mankato, MN: Capstone, 2008.

Summary: Scarecrows are useful to farmers and are a fun decoration for fall.

Action: Give everyone a little bit of straw before beginning the book. Ask them to hold the straw in both hands and hold out their arms. Can they stand still like a scarecrow through the whole book?

Action: Give everyone a white paper plate and some crayons. Ask everyone what they think a scarecrow face looks like. Ask them to draw their scarecrow face while you read the book. For added fun, cut eyeholes in the paper plate so the kids can use their scarecrow faces as a mask.

Jenkins, Steve. *Prehistoric Actual Size.*
Boston: Houghton Mifflin, 2005.

Summary: How big were the dinosaurs and other animals that lived at the same time? Some were so tiny that they could barely be seen, and others were so big that only a few of their teeth can fit in the book.

Action: Time for everyone to test out their size. Ask everyone to try to make themselves as small as the smallest animals in the book, then to try to make themselves super big. Adjust size for each animal. Be sure to save your best huge animal imitation for the forty-five-foot-long Giganoto-saurus.

Koontz, Robin. *Apples, Apples Everywhere! Learning about Apple Harvests.*
Illus. Nadine Takvorian. Mankato, MN: Picture Window Books, 2011.

Summary: Take a trip to an apple orchard to see the apple harvest and learn which ones are best to eat.

Action: Give everyone two plastic apples or two die-cut apples. Before you start reading, encourage everyone to hold their arms up like apple tree branches with ripe apples. When you get to pages 10–11, have everyone put their apples in a box at the front of the room, just like they do in the book.

Action: Pages 12–13 talk about apple worms. Give everyone a green or red paper plate with a couple holes cut into it (the holes should be big enough for little fingers to reach through). Also give everyone a small piece of yarn as their "worm." They can pull the worm through the apple holes just like a real apple worm.

Action: Sample apples! Pages 14–17 talk about tart versus sweet apples. Give everyone a small slice of each type to try. Which one do you like best? You might also wish to sample apple cider to coincide with pages 18–19.

Koontz, Robin. *Pick a Perfect Pumpkin: Learning about Pumpkin Harvests.*
Illus. Nadine Takvorian. Mankato, MN: Picture Window Books, 2011.

Summary: Autumn is here—it's time to pick the pumpkins. Go along with two friends as they learn how pumpkins grow and sample some delicious pumpkin pie.

Action: Give everyone an orange paper plate and a dark-colored crayon. If orange plates are not available, cut large circles out of orange construction paper. Explain that pumpkins are often used to make jack-o'-lanterns. While you read the book, everyone can make their own jack-o'-lantern.

Lendroth, Susan. *Old Manhattan Has Some Farms.*
Illus. Kate Endle. Watertown, MA: Charlesbridge, 2014.

Summary: The familiar song "Old MacDonald" is adapted to show how food can be grown in cities big and small.

Action: Instead of "E-I-E-I-O," this song repeats "E-I-E-I-Grow!" Everyone can reach their hands into the air to "grow" each time you sing that phrase.

Action: The verse about "Old Chicago" mentions basil, mint, chives, and dill. Bring in samples of each of these herbs for kids to touch and smell after singing that verse.

Lennie, Charles. *Tyrannosaurus Rex.*
Minneapolis: Abdo Kids, 2015.

Summary: Few dinosaurs garner as much interest and excitement as a T. rex. Minimal text accompanies photographs with lifelike-looking dinosaur models.

Action: Can you act like a Tyrannosaurus rex? Show everyone how to hold their elbows in tight to their body and walk around like a huge T. rex after each page.

Action: Extend the book by experimenting with T. rex arms: hold your elbows tight to your body and try to pick something up off of a table, or the floor. Make sure the item is something that would normally be very easy to pick up. Give everyone a chance to try out the experiment.

Lyon, George Ella. *All the Water in the World.*
Illus. Katherine Tillotson. New York: Atheneum Books for Young Readers, 2011.

Summary: Along with a message of conservation, this book spells out the water cycle in simple terms. Rather than reading like a textbook, the words crowd and bump and stampede as rain falls. Read this book aloud with expression to match the lively illustrations.

Action: Have a spray bottle of water ready. On any page where it rains, spray the storytime crowd with water.

Action: Hand out juggling scarves (or other pieces of fabric) before beginning the book. Tell everyone that the scarves are their umbrellas, and that they need to pay attention carefully and hold their umbrellas over their heads whenever it rains in the book. You can also hand out die-cut umbrella shapes for the kids to hold up.

Action: Everyone can pretend their fingers are droplets of water. When the water "swirls up," they can wiggle their fingers toward the sky. When it rains, they can hold their hands up high and slowly lower them while wiggling their fingers.

McReynolds, Linda. *Eight Days Gone.*

Illus. Ryan O'Rourke. Watertown, MA: Charlesbridge, 2012.

Summary: Four quick lines of poetic text per page show the Apollo 11 mission from launch to celebratory parade.

Action: Kids are fascinated with rockets and space exploration. Encourage everyone to act out some of the pages as you read the book:

- Countdown to blastoff. Be sure to countdown all the way from 10 to 1, then shoot your body up in the air.
- Put on your spacesuit.
- Step out of the *Eagle.*
- Walk on the moon.
- Put a flag in the ground.
- Splash down into the ocean.
- Wave to the people at the parade.

Neuman, Susan B. *Hop, Bunny! Explore the Forest.*

Washington, DC: National Geographic, 2014.

Summary: Take a bunny-guided hopping trip through the forest to see trees, deer, and wild turkeys.

Action: Hop with the bunny every time you hear the word "hop."

Action: Tape Popsicle sticks to die-cut bunnies so everyone can make their bunny hop along with the bunny in the book. Add a cotton ball as a tail to add texture and fun.

Action: Give everyone a few pieces of blue ribbon that have been tied together at one end. When you read the page about the bunnies hopping by waterfalls, show everyone how to hold their ribbon pieces at the top of their heads so that the "water" falls over their face.

Posada, Mia. *Guess What Is Growing Inside This Egg.*

Minneapolis: Millbrook, 2007.

> **Summary:** Can you guess what is growing inside each egg before the page is turned? There are clues in the text and, if you look closely, a clue in the illustrations as well.

> **Action:** Once each animal is revealed, take a couple seconds to move around like that animal. You might take this time to read the longer description of the animal, or leave that information for a curious family.

- Penguin: Waddle like a penguin.
- Alligator: Open your arms wide and snap them together like an alligator's jaw.
- Duck: Flap your hands as if they are duck feet swimming in the water.
- Sea turtle: Quickly crawl toward the sea.
- Spider: Quickly wrap up a bug in your silken threads.
- Octopus: Pretend each hand is a tiny octopus swimming in the water. Be sure to wiggle your finger "tentacles."

> **Action:** You can add to the previous action by using a song for each page:

> Tune: "Row, Row, Row Your Boat"
> Hatch, hatch, hatch, little egg, *(hold your fists together and break them apart like an egg hatching)*
> Show us what you hide. *(hide behind your hands)*
> Once you're done, we will play
> Like the animal inside. *(act like the animal that hatches out of the egg)*

Rustad, Martha E. H. *Leaves in Fall.*

Mankato, MN: Capstone, 2008.

> **Summary:** The changing leaves of fall are described through minimal text and shown in large photographs.

> **Action:** Give everyone a die-cut paper leaf. Vary the colors so that participants have a red, orange, yellow, or brown leaf. The different colors are referenced throughout the book. Whenever a specific color is mentioned, ask participants with that leaf color to hold it high in the air. This is a great way to learn about colors while learning about leaves.

> **Action:** Give everyone five to ten die-cut paper leaves. When you get to page 16, ask everyone to throw their leaves up in the air and watch them

fall. Be sure to step on the leaves once they hit the ground and make a crunching noise.

Action: Give everyone a copy of the tree outline from the appendix and a red, orange, yellow, or brown crayon (or all four). Ask them to decorate their fall tree as you read the book. Don't forget to draw some fallen leaves on the ground around the tree.

Rustad, Martha E. H. *Snowflakes.*
Mankato, MN: 2009.

Summary: What is snow? And how can we play in it? Minimal text and full-page photographs explain this natural phenomenon in simple terms.

Action: There are lots of things to do when it snows. Once you get to page 14, act out the snow activities with the book:

- Pretend to shovel snow.
- Pretend to build a snowman.
- Hold on tight to your sled as you zoom down a hill.

Action: If your location allows food, make a snow cone for everyone to taste "snow." You can use a blender to crush the ice and frozen concentrated juice to flavor it.

Action: Feel the cold. Read this book outside on a warm summer day (the hotter the better). Give everyone an ice cube to hold and play with while you read the book. This is a fun way to cool down and learn about snow. Remember: ice cubes are not snowballs—no throwing!

Sayre, April Pulley. *Go, Go, Grapes! A Fruit Chant.*
New York: Beach Lane Books, 2012.

———. *Let's Go Nuts! Seeds We Eat.*
New York: Beach Lane Books, 2013.

———. *Rah, Rah, Radishes! A Vegetable Chant.*
New York: Beach Lane Books, 2011.

Summary: Celebrate fruits, vegetables, or seeds in all their crunchy and colorful glory. Cantaloupe, plums, apples, even rambutans are in the fruit book. Photographs of vegetables from carrots to sweet corn to bok choy are featured alongside a rhyming list. The *Nuts* book boasts soybeans, walnuts, wheat, and quinoa.

Action: These books are meant to be read to a rhythmic chant. Include everyone by reading a page, then encouraging everyone to repeat it back to you. Be sure to add some cheerleading movements to the chant.

Action: Create an instrument using seeds. You can put seeds in between two paper plates, staple the sides together, and shake away. You can also put seeds inside an empty paper towel or toilet paper roll, and seal the edges with paper and tape. Play the instruments to a beat as you read along. Be careful to use seeds without allergy issues (no nuts).

Action: Vegetables get a bad rap, but they can be delicious. Pause after each page and ask everyone to raise a hand if they like the vegetables on that page. You can do the same thing with the fruit book (although the options are so eclectic that there may be many that no one in storytime has tried).

Sayre, April Pulley. *Raindrops Roll.*

New York: Beach Lane Books, 2015.

Summary: Close-up photographs show rain falling on plants and animals. The text is sparse, with some pages featuring only two words.

Action: Fill a spray bottle with water. The rain is falling on five double-page spreads of this book. Spray the storytime crowd with water after reading each of those pages.

Action: A photograph of a spider and her web is featured on two pages in this book. Pause reading on each of those pages to sing "The Itsy-Bitsy Spider" together.

Serafini, Frank. *Looking Closely around the Pond.*

Tonawanda, NY: Kids Can Press, 2010.

———. *Looking Closely inside the Garden.*

Tonawanda, NY: Kids Can Press, 2008.

———. *Looking Closely in the Rain Forest.*

Tonawanda, NY: Kids Can Press, 2010.

———. *Looking Closely through the Forest.*

Tonawanda, NY: Kids Can Press, 2008.

Summary: Can you tell what the picture is by seeing just a small portion? Guess and learn about plants and animals in the pond, garden, rain forest, or forest.

Action: There are five animals and four plants featured in *Looking Closely in the Rain Forest* (the other three titles contain similar arrangements). Create obvious movements for each—for example, shake your whole body for "animal" and stand completely still for "plant." As you read each page with "Look very closely. What do you see?," have everyone try to guess if the picture is of an animal or a plant by doing the correct movement before you turn the page.

Action: To make it a noisy guessing game, give everyone two different instruments. Have them play the instrument that corresponds with their guess. You may need to remind them on every page: "Shake the maraca if you think it's an animal. Shake your bells if you think it's a plant."

Shea, Susan A. *Do You Know Which Ones Will Grow?*

Illus. Tom Slaughter. Maplewood, NJ: Blue Apple Books, 2011.

Summary: We know a duckling can grow into a duck, but can a car grow into a truck? When read with expression, this book can be a humorous look at things that grow and things that don't. Flaps and foldout pages add to the appeal.

Action: Start out bent low to the ground, then stand up tall to "grow" for everything that does grow. Stay low to the ground for things like cars and washcloths that do not grow.

Action: Rather than using your entire body (like the above action), hold your open palms together and move your hands apart for things that grow.

Action: Use a prop—anything that can "grow" like a piece of ribbon or string or a piece of paper folded accordion style. Give a prop to everyone in storytime. Ask them to lengthen out the prop to signify "growth" for the objects in the book that can grow.

Stewart, Melissa. *Under the Snow.*

Illus. Constance R. Bergum. Atlanta: Peachtree, 2009.

Summary: Find out how animals survive the winter months in a field, forest, pond, and wetland. Watercolor illustrations portray ladybugs, a woodchuck, a carp, red-spotted newts, and other animals as they are mentioned in the text.

Action: A simple way to add movement to this text is by crossing your arms over your body and shivering at the end of each page. You can make the movements more complex by acting like some of the animals in the text:

- Pack close together like ladybugs.
- Pretend to tunnel through the snow like voles.
- Rest your head on your hands to nap with the chipmunk.
- Stay completely still and quiet like the centipede and the bumblebee queen.
- Curl up in a ball like the woolly bear caterpillar.
- Swim very slowly with the bluegills.
- Pretend to pull into a shell like the turtle.
- Pretend to munch on sticks like a beaver.
- Dart around like a red-spotted newt.

Action: Make copies for all storytime participants of the ladybug, beaver, or turtle outline in the appendix (or find an image of another animal from the book). Give each child a glue stick and cotton balls. Have everyone glue cotton "snow" to the animal.

Action: Give everyone white confetti before beginning the book. Let everyone toss the confetti up in the air to simulate snow at the beginning of the book. You may find that kids play in the "snow" while you are reading the book. Be eco-friendly by making confetti out of scrap or used copy paper. Make clean-up a breeze by asking everyone to help the snow "thaw" (pick up the pieces of paper) when spring arrives at the end of the book.

Stewart, Melissa. *When Rain Falls.*

Illus. Constance R. Bergum. Atlanta: Peachtree, 2008.

Summary: What do the animals in the forest, field, wetland, and desert do when it starts to rain? The watercolor illustrations add a sense of wetness to the book.

Action: Encourage everyone to help make rain fall on all the animals in the book. Whenever you hear the word "rain," slowly lower your hands while fluttering your fingers as if they are raindrops.

Action: Some animals take cover while others simply ride out the rain wherever they are. Give everyone a piece of fabric or a piece of paper—something they can use as shelter from the rain. Pay attention to each animal. Is it hiding in shelter? Hold your piece of fabric or paper above your head. Is the animal letting the rain fall on them? Hold your piece of fabric or paper down by your waist. Most animals seek shelter; the exceptions in this book are squirrels (although they pull their tail over their heads), hawk, ladybug, turtles (however they do pull their heads into their shells), whirligig beetles, ducks, and spadefoot toads.

Taback, Simms. *Simms Taback's Dinosaurs.*
Maplewood, NJ: Blue Apple Books, 2012.

Summary: Can you guess the dinosaur before all of the flaps are lifted? Learn a couple brief physical traits of Brachiosaurus, Triceratops, Pteranodon, Ankylosaurus, Stegosaurus, and, everyone's favorite, Tyrannosaurus rex. The flaps open to reveal a large, colorful illustration of each featured dinosaur.

Action: Add a movement to signify each of the dinosaurs:

- Brachiosaurus: Stretch out your neck to be long like this dinosaur.
- Triceratops: Use your hands to make horns on your head.
- Pteranodon: Stretch out your arms like wings and fly.
- Ankylosaurus: Make your hand into a fist and pretend it is the end of your tail.
- Stegosaurus: Hold your fingers out wide and put your hand behind your back to give yourself pointy plates.
- Tyrannosaurus rex: Show your big teeth.

Trueit, Trudi Strain. *Rainy Days.*
New York: Marshall Cavendish Benchmark, 2010.

Summary: Written partially in rebus form, this book tells us all the good things rain can do, from making the grass green to making the strawberries ripe.

Action: Give everyone a few long pieces of blue ribbon or blue yarn. They can use the ribbon or yarn to make rain in storytime. Most of the time kids can make general rain by holding the ribbon on one end and shaking it. On the page with the boots and hat, have them rain on their feet and heads.

Action: Encourage good listening skills. Ask participants to flutter their fingers like it is raining every time you say the word "rain."

Trueit, Trudi Strain. *Windy Days.*

New York: Marshall Cavendish Benchmark, 2010.

Summary: Written partially in rebus form, this book shows what happens on a windy day. The trim size is small, but the photographs are large: kites flying, windmills spinning, and trees bending.

Action: Pretend your storytime space is windy by twirling juggling scarves or ribbons in the air at the end of each page.

Action: Use juggling scarves to mimic the photos on each page of the book:

- Wrap the scarf around your shoulders like a coat.
- Hold the scarf high up to pretend it is a cloud.
- Hold the scarf tight and tall between two hands. Then bend it to one side to pretend it is a bending tree.
- Throw all the scarves up in the air then let them fall like leaves.
- Snap the scarf like a flag whipping in the wind.
- Hold the scarf high in the air then run around like it's a kite.
- Blow on the scarf to pretend you are the wind pushing a sailboat.
- Hold the scarf in one hand and twist it in circles like a windmill.
- Put the scarf on your head like a hat.

Action: If you have a small group and a large fan, you can add a quick extension activity to this title. Turn on the fan and let everyone take a turn holding their scarf in front of the fan, then letting go to watch it blow away.

Ward, Jennifer. *What Will Hatch?*

Illus. Susie Ghahremani. New York: Walker Books for Young Readers, 2013.

Summary: What will hatch from each of these different eggs? Turn the page to find out. Cutouts in the pages add another interesting element to the illustrations.

Action: Give everyone a plastic egg. As each animal hatches from its egg, ask them to break apart the plastic egg. Plastic eggs can be difficult to put back together (even for adults), so you may wish to ask kids to just hold the pieces together for all the subsequent animals.

Action: Eggs come in all shapes and sizes (as is illustrated by the book). Give everyone a copy of the egg outline from the appendix and a crayon. As you read the book, ask everyone to draw an animal inside their egg. What do they think will hatch from their egg?

Action: Pretend to act like each of the animals that hatches?

- Sea turtle: Use your hands like flippers as you crawl along the sand to the water.
- Penguin: Curl up on daddy's feet.
- Tadpole: Keep your legs together as if they are a long tail and pretend to swim.
- Crocodile: Open your arms wide and *snap*!
- Robin: Say "cheep-cheep-cheep" like you want a worm dinner.
- Caterpillar: Pretend to crawl along some leaves.
- Platypus: Swim in the water.

Werner, Sharon, and Sarah Forss. *Alphasaurs and Other Prehistoric Types.*
Maplewood; NJ: Blue Apple, 2012.

> **Summary:** Dinosaurs from A to Z are illustrated, using just the first letter of their name. Quick facts and a helpful pronunciation guide are provided on each page.
>
> **Action:** Many preschoolers are starting to learn letters and can recognize their favorite ones in print. Use this book over many weeks by focusing on just a couple of pages a week. Give everyone a die-cut of each letter that you will be looking at that week. While you share the facts from each page, they can trace the letter with their finger.

Ziefert, Harriet. *One Red Apple.*
Illus. Karla Gudeon. Maplewood, NJ: Blue Apple Books, 2009.

> **Summary:** Watch the life cycle of an apple from fruit to market to core to tree.
>
> **Action:** Cut open an apple (or two) so that kids can see the seeds inside. Depending on your group, pass the apple halves around so kids can get a closer look.
>
> **Action:** Share apple slices for everyone to eat on the page with the young girl enjoying an apple.
>
> **Action:** The word "apple" appears eleven times in the text of the book. Give everyone a die-cut apple and encourage good listening skills by asking them to hold their apple high in the air every time they hear the word.

the world around us

Abramson, Beverley. *Off We Go!*

Plattsburgh, NY: Tundra Books, 2006.

Summary: Photographs of children exploring the ways they can move are accompanied by simple descriptors of the pictures.

Action: This book just calls you to move along with it. Skip, hop, twirl, and tumble along with the kids the book. Do a movement for every page or just a few favorites.

Ajmera, Maya, Elise Hofer Derstine, and Cynthia Pon. *Music Everywhere!*

Watertown, MA: Charlesbridge, 2014.

Summary: See photographs of children around the world playing instruments, singing, and dancing to music.

Action: Play fun instrumental music while you read this book. Follow along when the book talks about particular ways to enjoy music:

- Clap your hands and stomp your feet.
- Sing "la la la."

- Pretend to play an instrument.
- Strum a guitar.
- Shake a pretend maraca.
- Bang a drum.
- Jump to the beat.

Action: Give everyone a quiet instrument to play while you read the book. For example, you can hand out paper plates and everyone can pretend the plates are drums while you read. You can also encourage everyone to pat their hands on the ground in front of them instead of handing out "drums." Be sure to pick something that won't be so loud that you cannot read over the noise. With a slightly older group, you may wish to have everyone play to the same beat.

Ajmera, Maya, Elise Hofer Derstine, and Cynthia Pon. *What We Wear: Dressing Up around the World.*

Watertown, MA: Charlesbridge, 2012.

Summary: People around the world wear special clothes for festivals, to be on a team, or to go to school. Photographs show kids from around the world in their special clothes.

Action: Give everyone a copy of the person outline from the appendix and some crayons. While you read the book, ask them to draw a special outfit on their person.

Action: Give everyone a mask before beginning the book. They can be partial masks like people wear at a masquerade ball or simple ones made by cutting holes in paper plates. On the page that talks about painting faces and wearing masks, have everyone put on or hold up their mask for the rest of the book.

Ajmera, Maya, Sheila Kinkade, and Cynthia Pon. *Our Grandparents: A Global Album.*

Watertown, MA: Charlesbridge, 2010.

Summary: Photographs from around the world and minimal text describe the special bond between a grandparent and grandchild.

Action: Give everyone a piece of paper and some crayons. While you read the story, they can draw a picture of their grandparents. This is especially nice to do around Grandparents Day (the first Sunday after Labor Day in the United States) because the kids can give the picture as a gift.

Carr, Aaron. *The Police Station.*

New York: AV2 by Weigl, 2014.

> **Summary:** The police are an important part of any neighborhood. Find out who the police are and how they can help.
>
> **Action:** It's never too early to teach kids to think of the police as friendly people who can help them. At the end of every page, wave and say hello to the police pictured on that page.
>
> **Action:** Have kids pretend to drive a police car after reading pages 12–13, and to be sure to make a nice loud siren noise.
>
> **Action:** If you have a small enough group, let everyone practice asking a police officer for help. Use paper to create a police badge that you can pin to your clothing. After reading page 16, which talks about going to the police if you are lost or hurt, allow everyone to take a turn talking to you like they need help. This may require some prompting: "Are you lost?" "Do you need help finding your mommy?"

Clay, Kathryn. *Tap Dancing.*

Mankato, MN: Capstone, 2010.

> **Summary:** Enter the studio and learn some of the basics of tap dance.
>
> **Action:** Pages 14–19 give simple instructions on how to hop, brush, and shuffle. Encourage the group to practice these moves along with the kids in the book.
>
> **Action:** Ask everyone if they can imitate the dancers on each page. Strike a pose to match the photographs.

Haley, Amanda. *3–2–1 School Is Fun!*

New York: Children's Press, 2010.

> **Summary:** See how much fun can be had in preschool when you play with blocks, make music, have lunch, go to storytime, and finger paint. This book is small in trim size but big in generating excitement about school.
>
> **Action:** The chant "3–2–1 / our school is fun" is repeated numerous times in the text. Create movements to go along with the chant. A fun example is standing up tall and slowly crouching down as you say "3–2–1." Then blast off for "our school is fun!"

Heling, Kathryn, and Deborah Hembrook. *Clothesline Clues to Jobs People Do.*

Illus. Andy Robert Davies. Watertown, MA: Charlesbridge, 2012.

Summary: Their laundry is hanging on the line. Can you guess their job based on their clothes? This book is a fun look at mail carriers, farmers, chefs, artists, carpenters, firefighters, and astronauts.

Action: Pretend to put on each item of clothing hanging on the line before guessing the occupation. For example, button up your shirt, put on your pants, and place the cap on your head for the mail carrier.

Jordan, Christopher. *Baseball Opposites.*

Plattsburgh, NY: Fenn/Tundra, 2014.

Summary: Unlike a typical opposites book, this title shows ones that are specific to the game of baseball. Readers will see a small baseball and a big stadium, a quick swing for a home run and a slow swing for a bunt, and more.

Action: Act out as many of the pages as possible:

- Make yourself small like a baseball then big like a stadium.
- Pretend to swing a bat quickly then slowly (be careful of your neighbor).
- Pretend to put on your uniform and batting helmet.
- Use your hands and arms to mimic opening and closing a stadium roof.
- Shiver in the cold cities and fan yourself in the hot cities.
- Pretend to swing a bat like a lefty and a righty.
- Pretend to catch a fly ball and a grounder.
- Sit on the bench then stand on the field.
- Make the umpire's call for safe and out.

Action: Give everyone a pom-pom or a soft ball. Act out the pages related specifically to a baseball:

- Throw the pom-pom high in the air for a pop fly.
- Roll it on the ground for a grounder.
- Throw it as far as you can for a home run.
- Throw it a short distance for a bunt.

Kerley, Barbara. *The World Is Waiting for You.*

Washington, DC: National Geographic, 2013.

Summary: Part inspirational mantra, part photographic journey of the planet, this book offers few words and lots of opportunity for discussion and dialogic reading.

Action: Take your time with this book, talk about the photographs and how everyone can become part of the picture:

- Look out a window (a real one if possible).
- Play follow the leader and walk along a path together. Where might this path lead?
- Spray the group using a bottle of water.
- Pretend to dive and swim with a dolphin and big fish. Ask, "Where do you think they are going?"
- Show everyone your dirty, icky hands. Ask, "Where have you been playing?"
- Dig in the dirt. Ask, "Have you found anything interesting?"
- Trace the path of a falling star with your finger.
- Blast off into space.
- Make yourself as big as you can. Ask, "Are you as big as the mountain?"
- Pretend to climb up a rope. Don't look down!
- Toss a starfish back into the water.
- Hold your hands up to your eyes as you peek into a small hole.
- Climb over huge crystals.
- Run toward the water.
- Paddle your kayak through the rapids. Sway back and forth with your boat.
- Blow out air to make wind.
- Hold on tight to your parachute. Ask, "What can you see from way up here?"
- On the last page, move however you want. (You may want to save this as the last book in storytime and use this page as a way to end the program.)

Action: Can you pretend to take the photographs in the book? At the end of each page, ask everyone to hold up a pretend camera to take a picture. Don't forget to focus and zoom. Click!

Kerley, Barbara. *You and Me Together: Moms, Dads, and Kids around the World.*

Washington, DC: National Geographic, 2005.

> **Summary:** Lyrical text and photographs showcase the bonds between parent and child around the world.
>
> **Action:** Encourage everyone to express their family bonds while you read this book aloud. Play instrumental music lightly in the background while parents and children dance together.
>
> **Action:** The words "me and you" are seen many times throughout the book. Encourage families to sit together so that kids and parents can point to themselves and then their family members each time the words appear. This boosts family bonds and listening skills.

Loewen, Nancy, and Paula Skelley. *Clothing of the World.*

North Mankato, MN: Capstone, 2016.

> **Summary:** Bright, colorful photographs show people around the world in different types of clothes. The photos are accompanied by simple, rhyming text.
>
> **Action:** Give everyone a copy of the person outline from the appendix and some crayons. Ask them to draw clothes on the person while you read the book.
>
> **Action:** Give everyone a juggling scarf or piece of fabric. Ask them to pretend it is a piece of clothing and add it to their outfit. They can also use the scarf to mimic clothing in the book, using it as a hat or a shoe.

Loewen, Nancy, and Paula Skelley. *Homes of the World.*

North Mankato, MN: Capstone, 2016.

> **Summary:** People live in many different types of homes. Some live in high-rises, some live in tents. Some live in old homes, some live in new homes. Take a photographic journey to visit homes around the world.
>
> **Action:** Give everyone a piece of paper and a crayon before beginning the book. While you share the book, they can draw a picture of their house. At the end of the book, ask everyone to hold up their picture for everyone to see.
>
> **Action:** The words "home" and "homes" appear eleven times in the text of this book. Teach everyone the sign for home in American Sign Language. Use a site like Signing Savvy (www.signingsavvy.com) for help (a

good way to remember the sign is that a home is a place where you eat and sleep). Encourage good listening skills by asking everyone to make the sign every time they hear the words "home" or "homes."

Martin, Isabel. *A Library Field Trip.*
North Mankato, MN: Capstone, 2015.

Summary: What happens at the library? Take a quick tour with this book.

Action: Take a tour of your own library while reading this book. Visit all the places mentioned and read the corresponding page. You can read the pages in order, or structure your tour based on what physically makes sense and read the pages out of order.

Action: After reading the book, give everyone in storytime a chance to be a librarian. They can take turns sitting in your special storytime chair. Or, if space and time allow, they can all check out their own books from behind the circulation desk.

Murphy, Liz. *A Dictionary of Dance.*
Maplewood, NJ: Blue Apple Books, 2007.

Summary: From "arabesque" to "zones," go through the alphabet to learn words associated with dance. A short description is provided for each word.

Action: Everyone can act out many of the words in this book. Pause to do all of the following: arabesque, gallop, hula, jump, kick, ouvert, tap dance, warm up, and extension.

Action: The book refers to many different styles of dancing. When each of these styles is mentioned, pause reading and play some appropriate music so everyone can dance: break dancing, dragon dance, folk dance, hula, quickstep, and tap dance.

Action: Use this book around the Chinese New Year. Focus on the "D" page and give everyone a die-cut dragon. Pause a few moments to allow everyone to dance around the room with their dragon.

Nelson, Maria. *Saying Please and Thank You.*
New York: Gareth Stevens, 2015.

Summary: Part of the Minding Our Manners series, this book is small in trim size but big in learning to be polite.

Action: Use Signing Savvy (www.signingsavvy.com) or another resource to learn how to say "please" and "thank you" in American Sign Language.

Teach these two signs to everyone before you start reading the book. Then, whenever you read either of those words, pause to sign it.

Schuette, Sarah L. *Birthday Customs around the World.*
Mankato, MN: Capstone, 2010.

Summary: Did you know Brazilians tug on their ear to celebrate their birthday? And Chinese eat long noodles? Learn some of the customs celebrated around the world.

Action: Pretend to act out the customs described in the book:

- Blow on a pretend noisemaker (or give everyone a real one to play with).
- Pretend to eat pancakes.
- Pretend to slurp noodles.
- Hit a pretend piñata.
- Tug on your earlobe.
- Put butter on your nose.
- Put on your new clothes.
- Clap.

Action: Sing "Happy Birthday" at the end of the book to show how we celebrate in the United States. Don't forget to blow out pretend candles.

Schuh, Mari. *All about Teeth.*
Mankato, MN: Capstone, 2008.

Summary: Parts of teeth, types of teeth, and how to keep them healthy are all explained in only a couple sentences per page.

Action: Pages 8–11 talk about the different types of teeth. Pause to feel your sharp front teeth and wide back teeth using your finger.

Action: On page 16, Lee uses floss to clean his teeth. Give everyone a long piece of ribbon. Have them pretend that their feet are teeth and show them how to "floss" with the ribbon to keep them clean.

Action: On page 18, Lee visits the dentist. Practice opening your mouth wide for a dentist visit.

Action: Give everyone a copy of the mouth outline from the appendix and a crayon. Ask them to draw teeth inside their healthy mouth.

Sterling Children's Books. *My First Basketball Book.*

New York: Sterling Children's Books, 2005.

Summary: This board book teaches twenty basketball terms, from "jersey" to "coach" to "layup." Each page features the term and a defining photograph.

Action: It's time to play. You can read this book as if you are a sports announcer and let everyone be part of the game. The words in quotations are a suggested script, but you should do what feels natural to you. The team names are also just suggestions; you may want to use team names that are local to your area:

"All right, folks, the teams are putting on their shoes and jerseys." *(everyone can pretend to do the same)* "Make sure your laces are nice and tight."

"The Cat and Dog teams are at their bench."

"Here come the referees and the coaches. Let's give them a big round of applause."

"The court is ready and the first Cat is dribbling the ball." *(pretend to dribble a basketball)*

"He shoots!" *(pretend to toss the ball into a basket)* "Swish!"

"Oh no. The Dogs just stole the ball. She's passing it to her teammate!" *(pretend to pass a basketball)*

"She's shoots and misses. The Cats get the rebound. He is rushing down the court. Look at that layup!" *(pretend to do a layup)*

"The Dogs have the ball back. Did you see that foul? The ref did. It's a free throw attempt for the Dogs. She's lining up at the free-throw line. She's bouncing the ball. She tosses it up. Basket!" *(line up at the line, pretend to bounce the ball, and toss the ball in)*

"The Cats have the ball back. They try for a jump shot . . " *(jump while tossing a pretend basketball)*

"The Dogs got the rebound. It looks like she's going for it! Dunk!" *(raise your hands above your head celebrating your dunk shot)*

"That's the game, folks. Join us next time here at *(library name)* Square Gardens."

Weatherford, Carole Boston. *Before John Was a Jazz Giant: A Song of John Coltrane.*

Illus. Sean Qualls. New York: Henry Holt, 2008.

> **Summary:** A vibrant and colorful ode to the musically rich childhood of John Coltrane.
>
> **Action:** Play a song by John Coltrane in the background while you read the story. If your library does not have any Coltrane CDs, you can play something off of YouTube. Encourage the kids to dance or pretend to play the saxophone while you read.

Willems, Mo. *Time to Say "Please"!*

New York: Hyperion Books for Children, 2005.

> **Summary:** A group of helpful, humorous mice help a young child learn how and why to say please.
>
> **Action:** Create a movement to go along with the word "please." Possibilities include the sign in American Sign Language or putting your hands together in prayer. Foster good listening skills by asking everyone to do that movement every time they hear "please" in the story.

art outlines

contents

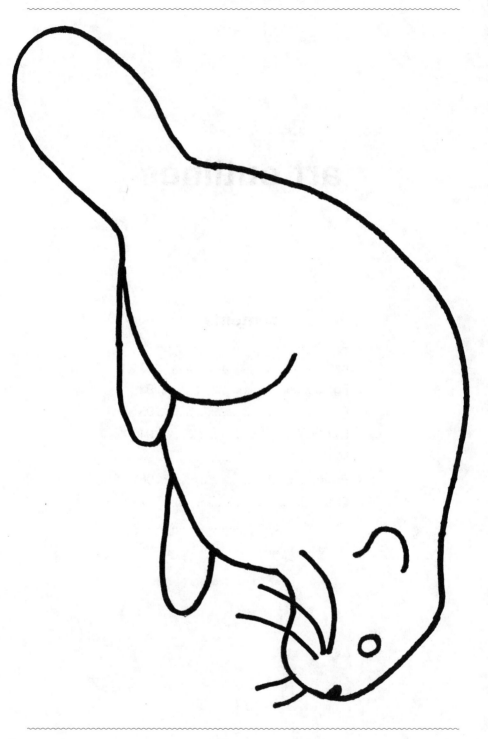

beaver

bird

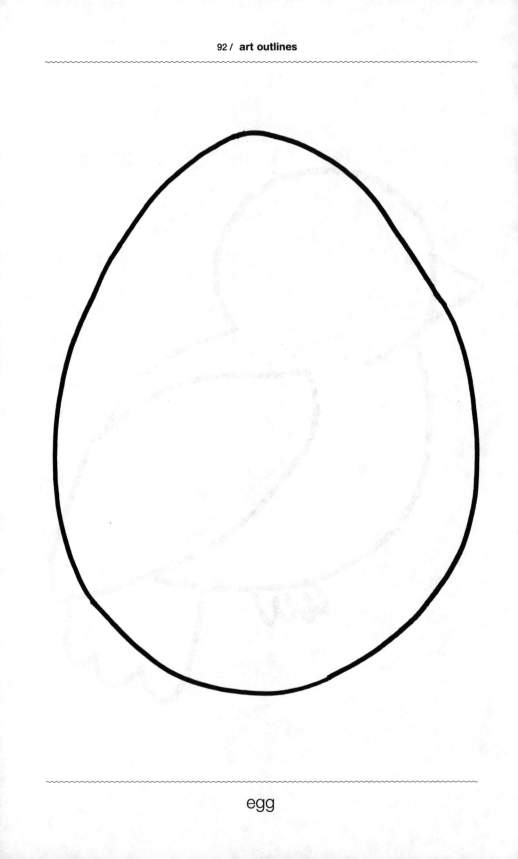

egg

fish

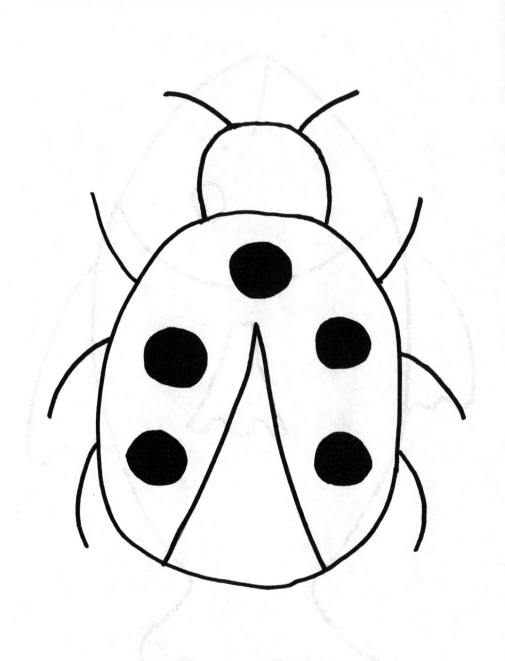

ladybug

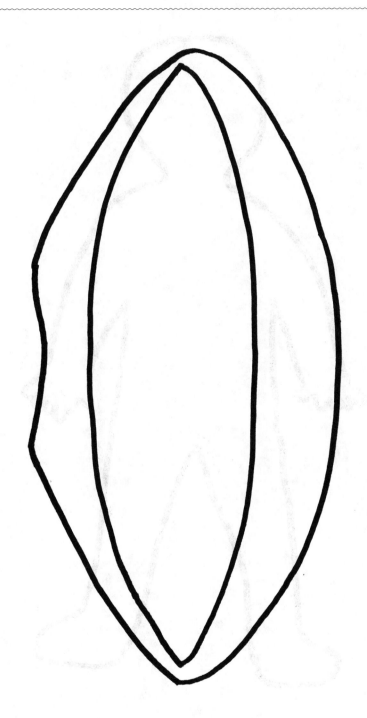

mouth

person

shark

tree

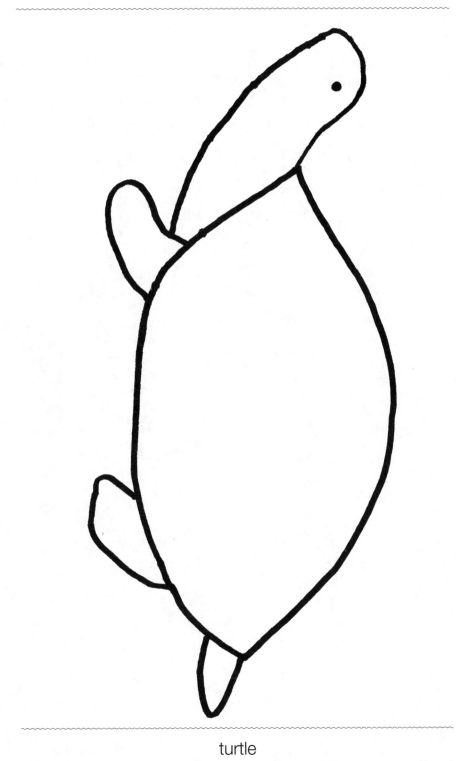

turtle

index by author

index by
storytime subject

index by title